Theme
and Variations

YEHUDI MENUHIN

Theme and Variations

𝔰𝔡

STEIN AND DAY/*Publishers*/New York

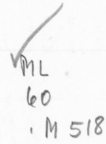

ML
60
. M 518

First published in 1972
Copyright © Yehudi Menuhin 1972
Library of Congress Catalog Card No. 70-186294
Printed in the United States of America
Stein and Day/*Publishers*/7 East 48 Street, New York, N.Y. 10017
ISBN 0-8128-1463-0

To my own
darling ~~Diana~~
whose presence
is the harmony
of my world.

Contents

PART THREE: THE ENVIRONMENT

PART FOUR: BRITAIN, EUROPE AND THE WORLD

List of Illustrations

Publisher's Foreword

IN RECENT YEARS Yehudi Menuhin has emerged as a striking spokesman for liberal values in modern society. He has had enlightening things to say not only on musical topics but also on a variety of other subjects. His interests range widely—from preventive medicine and the conservation of natural resources to the practice of yoga, from the education of children (both musical and general) to the politics of the Common Market. He loves painting, sculpture, poetry and architecture as well as music, and unlike many artists can also contribute to scientific discussion, and point to the connections between the arts and the sciences.

It seemed a great pity that the articles and essays written over the years should not be easily accessible in more permanent form. This volume represents a selection from Mr Menuhin's papers, including lecture material, some of which has been revised and adapted. Although the subject-matter ranges widely, from specialized chapters on musical topics to articles of more general interest, readers will find a linking thread throughout: the author's deep moral concern for the quality of life and his conviction of the essential unity of all experience.

Acknowledgements

THE AUTHOR and publishers wish to acknowledge that some of the essays and papers appearing in this book have been delivered as lectures or have previously appeared in print in various journals. Sources are given below.

'A Personal Introduction' first appeared as 'The Job that Got Away' in *Punch*, 2 June 1965. 'Music and its Public' was a message to the UNESCO Congress in Rome, organized by the International Music Council 1962. 'The Amateur Musician' was a message for the Standing Conference of Amateur Music. 'The Critics' Role' was an address to The Critics' Circle Dinner, 1962 and 'The Violin' was prepared for students at Dartington Hall Summer School of Music, August 1962. 'Improvisation and Interpretation' was a lecture given at London University in June 1963. 'Three Great Composers' originally appeared as (a) 'Bach': a translation of the Preface to a Facsimile Edition of Bach's Sonatas and Partitas; (b) 'Beethoven': a contribution to a Beethoven anthology prepared by the Akademie für Musik und Darstellende Kunst, Vienna; (c) 'Bartók': an article in *Music Magazine* published by Rockliff Publishing Corporation. 'Three Modern Masters': 'Georges Enesco' was adapted and expanded from a BBC broadcast; 'Pablo Casals' was a review of *Joys and Sorrows* by Pablo Casals and Albert E. Kahn (Macdonald 1970); 'Ravi Shankar' was the Introduction to *My Music, My Life* by Ravi Shankar (Simon and Schuster, New York 1968). 'The Compleat Education' is the revised text of the Loveday Lecture delivered at Bristol University, May 1962. 'The Teaching of the Young' was the Campbell-Orde Memorial Lecture, delivered at the Golden Lane Theatre, London, under the auspices of the Arts Educational Trust, on 25 November 1970. 'A Musical Education' was a lecture delivered at the University of London Institute of Education, 19 October 1966. 'Art and Science as Related Concepts' xiv *Acknowledgements*

is the revised text of a lecture delivered to the Royal Society. 'Heaven on Earth' was first published in *Resurgence*, Vol. 3 no. 1, May/June 1970. 'Architecture Today' was a contribution to a 'Think-In' sponsored by the School of Architecture, Architectural Association, 17 July 1967. 'The Indian Contribution' formed part of a speech made at the presentation ceremony of the Nehru Award, 4 November 1970. 'Cultural Influences of Empire' was a paper read to a joint meeting of the Royal Society of Arts Commonwealth Section and the Royal Commonwealth Society on 16 February 1967. 'The World Citizen' is based on a BBC broadcast.

Theme
and Variations

A Personal Introduction

'WHAT,' said the questionnaire, 'finally decided you to specialize in your particular field? Chance or clear-cut decision?' Then, very casually laying a trap: 'Money or what?' The 'or what' one imagined was the camouflaging leaves over the pit . . . 'Would you,' it continued jovially, 'have actually preferred a different job?' and then, pinning one down suddenly, 'And if so, what?'

Beautiful images presented themselves of a variety of eminences facing the succinct questions . . . Canon Collins for example? 'All my life since I was a toddler I've longed to be a tenor. Not one of your tuppenny-ha'penny tenors, but one of those who would hold a vast house spellbound as he hit the top note in a beautiful worshipful silence to be broken only by a cascade of rapturous applause. But there was no money in my vocal cords and my teeth were the wrong shape, so I turned to the Church.'

Marlene Dietrich? 'My family had me all set for the Heilsarmee, but I could never sing "Ein Feste Burg" in tune . . .' and so on and so forth . . . But then one was only avoiding the issue, funking looking back down the long tunnel of a career to try and find where the divergence might have occurred, what occasioned the choice—if indeed there ever had been one.

The trouble was that it meant such a long journey, at least forty-five of my forty-eight years, and one felt that if the journey were not made with extreme caution one might end slap up against a baby in a cradle.

The sounds had always been there; sounds to capture and arrange in sequences, together with a sense of order not so much dependent on concrete facts as upon abstract and invisible symbols whose absolute was always relative to the next symbol. Into this private and entirely satisfying world came other aspects of the unborn which are the kin of musical embryos, so that between

I

working at my first Mozart concerto (the one in A major which I am ashamed to say I treated very cavalierly, gobbling it up like so much corned beef in order to get to the *pièce montée*, the Beethoven), the mind would wander guiltily, exploring the possibility of a man-powered plane (was it the flight of those soaring cadenzas that prompted me or the longing of the seven-year-old to escape this tyrannical instrument? Was it the sense of solitude added to the captivity demanded of the violin that pushed me to design a Leonardoesque contraption that could mean escape without risk of losing that lovely solitude?): be that as it may I soon abandoned that slightly grandiose idea and got swept up by another.

I must have been a somewhat pedantic small boy. I was certainly a very plump one, so that why rattling along the dirt roads of the High Sierras on the way to a childhood picnic in our first old Dodge should have inspired me with a determination to invent a suspension-framed car, considering that no amount of bouncing could possibly have dented me, I don't know. But it certainly did, and the subsequent picnic became something to be got through at top speed till I could get home to pencil and paper and the first rough drawings of a body suspended by an umbilical cord from the centre of the chassis. It would have been a splendid thing, swinging gracefully like some broad-beamed nautch-girl, and I am sad to remember that I convinced nobody of the grace and practicability of my idea.

The habit of thinking inwardly in terms of things to be recreated probably goes hand in hand with invention, and mouldering among tattered old copies of such long laid-by works as the de Bériot concerto lie blueprints of hydraulic brakes (I may add modestly a good time before such appeared anywhere) and disc brakes, too, the latter obviously born of long and exhausting boyhood tours when nights in the train were rendered hideous by the screech of the clumsy shoe-brakes as the racing train would jerk itself in a series of spasms to a sudden halt, at least a dozen times between East Overshoe and Vinegar Bend.

And goodness alone knows what sleepless nights spent tossing on half a hundred marshmallow hotel and ship mattresses brought forth the conception of counterweighted beds that would, like a sailor's hammock, gently follow and trim the sleeper's movement however much he wriggled.

I suppose the very enclosedness of my life from so young an age, together with its early fulfilment, forced any excess mental energy to expend itself ever deeper over the same small area of experience, so that all my inventions tended to belong to travelling. And though in those far-off days of the late 1920s air travel was not yet the vast commercial enterprise it has since become, none the less my moving inner world had the sky full of planes and people crossing and intercrossing like teams and flocks of birds preparing for some perpetual winter migration.

And perhaps because the violin is such an autonomous instrument, tuned and retuned by the player, on which he for ever creates his own pitch, so my world was one of individuals coming to terms not so much with each other as basically with the law and order of nature, which underlies all things. But my job had me tightly in its grasp and although I did show one or two of my ideas to an occasional expert, and twice enjoyed the bitter satisfaction of learning that someone had only just superseded me by a few months, there never was sufficient opening of any branch road from the steady highway of my musical progression that would allow of anything but a backward glance, as though I had perceived from the corner of my fixed eye something white fluttering in a hedge, or some vista down an alley that was gone ere it was properly seen.

Would the job (if this longing to invent comes under that heading) have 'got away' had different pressures arisen to crystallize it into a more concrete possibility? And, conversely, can I say that I 'got into' my present one? Does the artist really ever know the 'how' or the 'when' of his polarization? It is surely hard enough to know the 'where', the direction, without bothering one's head about the reason why. In this way maybe all artists are some gigantic Tennysonian band of Light Brigaders, for ever doing or dying without questioning their fate, blissfully oblivious of the Raglans and the Cardigans, galloping about the Peninsula with only the faint hope of some Florence Nightingale at the backs of their woolly and devoted minds . . . ?

Anyway, I could not possibly fathom my own case, my whole process of thought being based on the iceberg principle: one-ninth maximum conscious and above, eight-ninths (minimum) sub-conscious and below, and even that quite often becomes an inverted pyramid with the instinctive neatly and conveniently upwards, so that I suspect I would anyway have found myself doing whatever it happened to be quite unintentionally, out of goodness knows what impulse of curiosity, doggedness and the ingrained desire to explore mainly elusive things.

And then, as I grew older, there came another influence, yet another set of ideas growing out of my narrow experience, for it was surely in the nursing of those colds, wrapped to the streaming eyes by anxious parents in layers of wool, in turn covering a whole armoury of burning mustard plasters brutalizing the germs away in order to get well enough for the next day's concert, haunted with the fear of blowing the bridge off the violin in one gigantic sneeze and ruining for ever the andante of the Beethoven Concerto—it was surely then that these occupational hazards awoke in me an ineradicable interest in and respect for medicine.

This, too, in its way, followed the precept of the individual finding his balance with nature, for all my boyhood I dreamed of an approach to medicine that would be mainly prophylactic rather than therapeutic, the spectacle of man yielding to and going along with nature rather than antagonizing and fighting her.

I used to wonder what sort of doctor I might have made as I stood long hours in operating theatres during the war, watching the unbelievable skill and patience of a Dickson Wright at work on a long and exquisitely handled piece of brain surgery. Would I have resembled the ex-musician turned surgeon, who, in the classic story, before a crowded audience of students applauding his ulcer operation, rewarded their appreciation of his skill by whipping out the poor patient's appendix as an encore?

I wonder? But my mind still wanders in these fields (so closely related to the disciplines and abstractions of music), with their re-creation and creation, and their fluid lines of demarcation offering a flexibility that makes of them an organic whole but an ever-mutable one. I wonder whether, had I been all three at the same time—doctor, inventor and violinist—I would have applied a pizzicato technique to the separating of adhesions and sewn them up with metal E-strings. Or had the inventor got the upper hand, whether I would have invented an undisturbably pitched violin constantly and permanently controlled by a thermostat embedded in the left ear-lobe; or to be more practical, and as the violinist does seem to have come uppermost so far, whether I should not bend my energies to inventing a computer into which a musician can feed all the music he is likely to play for his particular instrument and which, clapped to his temples by means of tiny electrodes, feeds into his mind and memory whatever his requirements be for that particular concert.

The unaesthetic appearance of such an apparatus could easily be overcome by wearing one of the now so fashionable wigs, whiskers, side-burns, fringes or Dundrearies, and no one in the audience would be one whit the wiser.

You may notice that I have so far avoided the Trap—the $64 'Money or What' question. It is simply that money to me has always been the greatest abstract of them all. Perhaps it springs from the good fortune of having had earning capacity since small boyhood and at the same time of not being cognizant of its amount or value that gives me this elliptical angle—that perhaps of a crab approaching the Bank of England at a fast pace through dense traffic?

For the inventor is always borrowing currency from the violinist, and from the prophylactic doctor, too, so that my schemes and projects swallow up the earnings in one perpetual circle, as though some three-headed Janus, watching what went out and went in and fell from above, were manipulating his dwindling funds from one pocket to the other, while the head in the centre, with the violin tucked firmly under its chin and its arms sawing away, wistfully watched the upturned hat on the pavement.

'Would I have preferred a different job?' No, I suppose, because I am, as much as it is possible to be, a free man, slave only to the instrument of my early choice, the violin.

1965

Part One: Music

1. Music and the Nature of its Contribution to Humanity

MUSIC CREATES ORDER out of chaos; for rhythm imposes unanimity upon the divergent, melody imposes continuity upon the disjointed, and harmony imposes compatibility upon the incongruous.

Thus as confusion surrenders to order and noise to music, and as we through music attain that greater universal order which rests upon fundamental relationships of geometrical and mathematical proportion, direction is supplied to mere repetitious time, power to the multiplication of elements, and purpose to random association.

It is no wonder that ancient sages sensed music in the movement of the heavenly spheres. Thus the fundamental relationship of one-to-one—as man to woman, or yin to yang—finds its audible rendering in musical form: exposition–recapitulation—a form which gradually extends around its seed to produce and embrace a content—the development section.

The more rapid frequencies find their musical counterpart in the tidal (as it were) increase and decrease in volume and in the contrasting characters of the musical elements. The physiological frequencies of breathing and pulse, of pressure and relaxation, of work and rest, find their musical counterpart in the basic pulse and counter-rhythms, in the rise and fall of a phrase and its interweaving counterpoint, and in the increase and decrease of tension.

The faster frequencies of pitch and the simultaneous sounds and changing relationships of notes at different pitches affect us deeply and irresistibly, as they penetrate and reveal the subconscious and the intangible. For only musical sound can communicate the intangible, the yearnings, aspirations, the sensations and moods of life—our other senses reveal the presence of

9

palpable objects and by the same token limit our vision, except as our mind and experience re-interpret them.

Music can be and is almost an *immediate* revelation, requiring little interpretative effort on the part of the initiated and submissive listener.

Sound waves can more deeply penetrate our subconscious—can more profoundly affect our emotions—than any other impressions. Man's ultimate leap, when approaching his God, is through music; man's ultimate release of exuberance can again be through music, from drinking songs to dances; he marches to war with blood-curdling drums in Africa and driving brass in European civilizations; he falls in love to music. Music serves the shepherd, as a companion in his solitude or to communicate with other shepherds, as it does the Tibetan lama, or the Sovereign of England, to solemnify great public ceremonies. Through music we share and become part of all great occasions. We are welded into one group, sharing each other's sense of sorrow or exhilaration.

Music can also reveal more penetratingly the nature of peoples alien to each other: our understanding for instance of the African temperament and character has come about more through their influence upon our daily music than through any intellectual, social or other contact.

In fact music begins where words end. It is the only medium which recalls us inescapably to that sea of creation and existence, the one infinity of which we are a fraction, but not the detached fragment we might be without music.

As humanity reaches out to this infinity, endeavouring to understand and—perhaps unforgivably—to control it, it finds itself ensnared in a trap of its own making; for it is the very faculty of rational enlightenment, that very reason that reveals the unity of which we are a part, that, for lack of another unspoken awareness such as faith or music, could sever us from that same unity.

For even reason, the most objective of all our gifts, is itself only a part of life and cannot engage or subject within its realm the living motives that lie outside its scope. To quote Pascal, 'le coeur a ses raisons que la raison ne connaît pas'—and Pascal's 'coeur' comprises for us today not only 'heart' but the subconscious memory of each moment of our mysterious evolution and history. Music is the river-bed which can guide and contain this powerful and eruptive flow coming from our subterranean levels of consciousness—a course which unites us with that ocean I speak of.

It is a wry commentary upon our age, which has so lavishly produced such fruits of reason as the myriad scientific disciplines, their tangible practical results in terms of power, means of communication and methods of multiplication, that the supreme fruit of reason (and heart) has so far eluded humanity at large—a balanced human being in a balanced society. It should however be no wonder, for it is this very arrogance, the apparent omnipotence of limited reason which refuses to recognize, to come to terms with and genuinely to embrace its counterpart—the heart as I described it.

Music today reflects this same estrangement, offering us more often than not either the dessicated abstract constructions of 'Meccano' composers—or the cheapest of sentimental trash crooned over the loudspeaker.

This is a dangerous and explosive situation—in which at any moment these two elements, the one dry as gunpowder and tinder, the other ungoverned and intense as flame, may touch each other off. For they exist together in the same person, and unless they are reconciled to each other, unless these two elemental qualities learn to coexist in harmony, the human being will always remain prey to prejudice, violence and barbarity.

Music, or somewhat more specifically the love of music, was considered by most people during that comparatively innocent era preceding Hitler and his Third Reich to be a sovereign barrier against barbarism, until the behaviour of this most musical, philosophical and rational of peoples finally and for ever shattered the illusion.

Music can indeed still be a refuge and an escape and can, just as the church or any other great and compelling house of worship, serve as a silent confessional to the prostrate listener, surrendering his own unwelcome identity, taken up and enveloped within a sea of sound waves, which successfully isolate him from both his own self within and the world without. But so long as the individual is merely using music, in a sense exploiting it, even this great and

noble art can enjoy only a limited effect—limited as much to place
and time as the momentary Sunday calm and propriety of some
witch-burning Puritan community. Only he or she who serves
his muse, who serves music (and today this no longer has an
exclusive connotation but must embrace music of many different
cultures, past and present)—only the one who can translate and
transfer the code of deep musical experience into ordinary
behaviour, into the reactions and reflexes of daily life, can find
his own thoughts and actions towards his fellow-man influenced in the direction of self-discipline, towards a form of
aesthetic morality and a more penetrating understanding of himself. Setting 'art' up on a pedestal, without suffering for and by
her, belonging to her, must remain both morally and socially an
utterly useless pursuit.

Today, when the human being, as in the past, is threatened
with exposure and imprisonment in a world regimented by impersonal demons of his own invention, forces economic, mechanical, social and spiritual, it is more than ever imperative to his
existence to restore him to a spontaneous and complete expression
of himself, preferably one achieved by himself and through his
own body as in singing and dancing, one built to *his own* measure,
serving his own biological entity, spiritual and physical, and
enveloping him and his community in as protective an environment of benign sensations as the silkworm's cocoon.

It is for these reasons that music today, liberated and spontaneous, holds out more hope for humanity than ever before.

Every child in something like a hundred schools in Hungary
begins his scholastic day singing Kodály and Bartók choruses. The
class read them at sight, write music on the blackboard by ear,
literally 'toning' themselves up with oxygen, invigorating their
whole spiritual, intellectual and psychological capacities with this
daily one-hour routine. Carl Orff in Germany brings to the
children there a synthesis of music, dancing, mime and words,
reduced to simple components that can be freely handled by the
very young.

Both these approaches are now spreading to England, Canada
and the United States. At McGill in Montreal and now at New
Paltz State University College in New York, as at the University
of California in Los Angeles, students are actually learning to

play the sitar of India and the gamelan of Bali with expert teachers, much as they would learn a foreign language and its literature and culture.

The United States is in the throes of a veritable revolution in school music-teaching. The cheap and trivial, the dull and academic musical materials are slowly giving way to musics from many periods and peoples, graded according to complexity and difficulty and performed with a real understanding of style by exhilarated children. Unesco has published many enlightening texts and recordings, which are an invaluable aid.

At the other end of this rainbow we find released the spontaneous improvisatory urge for self-expression and adventure in the various forms of impulsive sounds or noises produced by jazz groups and others, using ingeniously constructed instruments varying from sardine cans to steel barrels. Out of this has grown a tremendously heightened interest in all forms of music played directly from the performer's heart and mind, with no reference to the printed score, as is the case with all the music of India, Africa and the Far East, the Gipsies, the village fiddlers of Norway and Scotland, the bagpipe folk-songs and dances, and so on (aleatoric interludes in otherwise composed scores are an example of an effort to combine the composed and the improvised). This is a development utterly new to our world—the satisfaction through the deeper study of our own past and of our neighbour's, of a hunger long suppressed by the tyranny of the printed word, of the superficial and rigid, of the ukase, the *Verboten*, the dead hand of industrial slavery and middle-class bourgeois conformity, important as the latter is to stability and the 'homely' virtues.

No longer is it quite sufficient to hunt down and kill strange and wonderful animals in Africa, no longer should we wish both cannibalistically and symbolically to eat our victim's heart, or to sell it; today we begin to sublimate these urges by hunting with a camera, by learning tribal languages and communicating with birds and dolphins, by identifying ourselves intellectually, spiritually and aesthetically with those whose way of life differs entirely from ours—encouraging each other to be free and independent to express what is peculiar to each, rather than to count heads and trophies from the dead.

The urge is the same, but sublimated. It remains curiosity,

conquest, covetousness, even greed—but turned to life and not to death. This new later twentieth-century approach to music, even more than to painting, is perhaps one of the most promising avenues of human and humanistic evolution. I say music even more than painting, for music and sound occupies us quite literally, physically and spiritually, as it occupies time itself. As I said earlier, we are immersed in a living sea of sound from which there is no escape and which must (if well used) condition us more profoundly than might a purely visual art, which is more objective.

For this reason I find the recent imposition of 'canned' music supplied indiscriminately to airports, aeroplanes, restaurants, subways, harmful to the cause of music, rendering it simply a panacea masking an intolerable situation. It is as absolutely reprehensible in principle as it is revolting in practice. It is one thing to choose your particular music, to go to a dance hall or concert or restaurant: it is quite another to have it imposed upon you. On top of which this imposition is usually perpetrated by people with no taste and horrid equipment, and is inescapable. I believe this should be forbidden by law as an intrusion upon the privacy and dignity of the individual.

To return to a happier theme. One of the most fascinating institutions in the world is the International Institute for Comparative Music Studies and Documentation in West Berlin. It is amusing to compare this with its more primitive prototype. When I first came to Berlin as a boy of thirteen in 1929 I was taken to a famous noisy restaurant, enormous in size and containing many vast rooms, each of which represented some national style, with food, drink, decorations, costumes, music and dance to match. Now we can travel the whole world of music within a quiet villa in the suburbs of that same city, fulfilling cultural and human requirements undreamed of either in those days of my boyhood or the dulled, brown, barbaric and arrogant years to follow. And now it is possible to enrich the education of our children by drawing on the music and traditions of many cultures, and encouraging them to love and respect life in all its variety.

GSTAAD, 1966

2. Music and its Public

THE BASIC CULTURAL PROBLEM of our day is the rapid and sudden physical and intellectual emancipation of multiplying and overwhelming majorities: mass production literally —not only of cars and bottles, but of men as well—a quantitative process with a very strong bias towards uniformity.

Each man is no longer a single hand-made job but a standardized product—the result of influences commonly shared, of monopoly-minded propaganda either commercial, state or ideological; the result of a limited number of powerful pressures working upon a docile, uncommitted, flat and uniform material, like clay, sheet metal or printing paper. One might say that the creative act of impregnation is giving way to a robot process of stamping or transferring one negative mould to numberless positive images, as with the printing machine.

The cultural crisis is particularly acute when a specific image evolved in a given civilization, as, for instance, the urban American formula, is suddenly applied globally to the most diverse human material. Man is unable to assimilate or to identify himself organically with the new mould. Once severed from his own ancient roots, 'untimely ripped' as it were, he is then neither fish nor fowl, and remains insecure, dissatisfied, demanding, impatient and frustrated.

Fortunately we are dealing with man, who like the scorpion (and unlike the snake), conceals his ultimate defence in his tail —the very last limb in all respects and the last to be conditioned.

Man will for ever demand uniqueness and personal fulfilment. Whatever agonies and nightmares he has sustained over the past few thousand years, including our own era, he has never forfeited this dream even as he has never forfeited his longing for union with the infinite.

So far he has had, for the most part, to content himself with the

3. The Amateur Musician

As far as I know, in Biblical days there was little distinction between the amateur and the professional musician—in fact I suspect that these terms hardly applied at a time when, unlike in our present Western world, endeavour was not measurable in terms of money.

In India the great tradition that music and the dance, or for that matter learning, must not be used to earn money, is only now gradually ceding ground in the face of the subdivision of time, especially radio time. After all, we might at least gracefully grant the donor the right to give when the impulse seizes him; when he must give at definite and pre-ordained times he naturally demands pay! The musician, in spite of the great skill of his art, was not expected to be a professional in terms of earning capacity, but this kind of professionalism provides a good discipline all the same.

It is a happy thought, and encouraging, that in English-speaking countries the word 'amateur' can be used in its true sense of *amare*, to love, and if 'amateur' designates the one who out of a deep love gives of himself unstintingly, and if 'professional' is inferred to designate the opposite, give me the amateur each time.

Fortunately for musicians and for humanity, things are not nearly so black and white as our crude and arbitrary abstractions would imply. In fact, unless the professional were an amateur at heart, and unless the amateur received the good training and had the intelligence and the will necessary to achieve some command of his craft, we should have no music, and for that matter no art at all.

The amateur is the source of all culture and art. It is the peasant amateur who delights us with his violin and cimbalom, and whether in the palaces or in the apartments of Vienna and Budapest, or on the African veldt, the plantations of the New

World, the streets of Rio de Janeiro or New Orleans, it has always been the amateur around whom the living culture of the day grew up.

There is no such thing as music divorced from the listener. Music as such is unfulfilled until it has penetrated our ears. We can cultivate keen ears, ears ready to grasp the subtle in melody and rhythm. We can encourage the use of some instruments. Above all we can kindle the flame of self-expression, which must sing or dance, strum or beat a sound, or paint or draw some line or colour.

For this to happen we need to foster the kind of rhythm and repose in our activity which is transmutable in forms of spontaneous expression. The word 'leisure' today often merely denotes the absence of work. This in itself is purely negative and not transmutable into art. We must also try to find some way around that element of nihilism which springs from man's subservience to his machine. Who can sing in the shattering isolation of a tractor cab? What folk music would we have if all our forbears had ploughed, tilled and harvested to the accompaniment of its noisome and uninspiring stink? What rousing marching songs can we expect from a mainly mechanized army? The mechanical cotton-picker would have denied us a great part of our negro heritage in song. And to put, as it were, a final flourish to the extemporized, the loudspeakers in every conceivable corner see to it that any impulse towards musical self-expression is sandbagged, paralysing both mind and senses and brutalizing the hearer, turning him from a putative participator into a passive target.

I am grateful to every amateur who wishes to do something for himself without using some manufactured commodity. But to do so he must be inspired by the love of something living. No one to my knowledge has ever delivered himself of a tune while conscientiously contemplating a can of peas. One of these days (terrible thought), to fill the vacuum created by our atrophy we will no doubt have tin cans which play a tune as they are opened!

LONDON, 1954

4. New Music and Learning to Listen

PUBLIC INTEREST in contemporary music is essential to the composer, just as an intelligent reading public is essential to the author. The one could hardly exist without the other. The problem, however, of maintaining a high level of exchange between public and composer is extremely complex.

The composer shares the same difficulty as the audience, in that he must evolve and they must understand a 'new' language. It is almost more than can be asked of any audience to master the language and to read its message correctly at one and the same time. When we are looking for an aesthetic, or emotional, or moral impact we must at least partly understand the language in which we are addressed. The overwhelming majority among any audience looks mainly for inspiration and the reflection of familiar sentiments, thoughts and passions; they are not students in a classroom, striving after new knowledge.

We—composers and performers—must have a sympathetic understanding of the great effort required on the part of the public today. In the past, any given audience was immersed in a regional or a period style, and even the newest creations emerged from that style. Less mental effort was required to assimilate new works.

To cite an example, it has taken some years for the works of Bartók to command the respect and reverence they now receive. It was as recently as 1947 that my first performance of the 'First Sonata with Piano' evoked from isolated quarters of a packed Salle Pleyel shouts of 'Ridicule! Absurde!' and so forth. I played it there again some ten years later, when such a manifestation would have been utterly inconceivable. This does not mean that there are not still plenty of unconverted or unconvinced people amongst audiences, who are unable to appreciate this work. It simply means that a sufficient number do and that the 'tone' is

set, as it is in church. Bartók has been canonized. In many cases
where a work has intrinsic value and appeal, recordings, which
help to make the students and listener independent of the concert
hall, hasten this process.

Little-known or unknown works have in my experience always
acted as a stimulant to artist, audience and connoisseur alike. The
accelerated mental and emotional activity induced by the un-
familiar—if only at its lowest level of surprise—unfailingly
heightens by contrast the enjoyment of the familiar.

The performer should not give up the struggle, for his patience
and perseverance will be rewarded in the end. Aaron Copland is
quite right when he laments the sterility in the life of the 'run-of-
the-mill' virtuosi who, determined at all costs to achieve popular
careers, grind out the same hackneyed concertos day after day and
year after year. That even the Chinese now follow this practice
was shown by the extraordinarily brilliant and wonderful performance of the Rachmaninov 'Variation of the 24th caprice of
Paganini' played by a Chinese pianist whom I heard in Bucharest,
and who carried away the first prize at the inaugural Enesco
Concours then taking place in that city. I am happy to note,
however, that ever-increasing numbers of my colleagues are
giving more and more of their time to modern works.

Unlike sculpture, painting and writing, 'live' musical performances are dependent upon two intermediaries: the interpreter, who
represents the composer, and the impresario, who represents the
public. Where a capital city exists, traditionally representative of
its national culture and providing the major audiences of the
country, the managements are keen and aware of their responsibilities. But when a management has to work on a continental
scale, then, as with the films, very often the lowest common
denominator prevails. In this case it is important for the many
small local nuclei—as for instance museums, universities, associations of young men and young women—to become articulate and
link themselves loosely together, so that from a common head-
quarters they may procure those attractions not normally on a
manager's list.

In Moscow, which is the capital and (we may assume) the most
progressive city of the Union of Soviet Socialist Republics, the
works of Bartók, Bloch, Elgar, Enesco, Vaughan Williams,

Copland, for example, are still unperformed.[1] This compares ill
with musical activity in smaller areas—Finland, Norway, Poland,
or Southern California.

In all cities in Italy musical societies are a fine example of group
effort and provide a counterweight to the spontaneous and
luxuriant mass musical life of the country. They support music
handsomely and are, in fact, the continuation of the former
aristocratic patronage on a broader level. Thanks to these active
groups, Italy is leading the world in its performances of contemporary music.

Although it is evident from the foregoing that the public should
not remain passive and must be responsible for more than the
buying or failing to buy of tickets, the composer, or at any rate
most composers, cannot afford to live in an ivory tower. More
than one sort of responsibility rests upon them: the responsibility,
for example, of teaching and encouraging children. And the composer more than ever today must be one who thinks or senses
more intensely than others—he must be able to communicate his
visions and his truths, wrested from within himself. Just as a
dictionary is a thoroughly well-ordered work, but can convey no
message, so do certain of our exclusively cerebral contemporary
works seem mere glossaries of effects and inventions.

A composer who is exemplary in seeking to bridge the gap is
Benjamin Britten, who has done more for the education of
children in English schools than almost any other contemporary
British composer, and whose impulse comes from a spontaneous
and heartfelt understanding of children. Others include Béla
Bartók and Zoltan Kodály in Hungary, and Villa-Lobos in Brazil.

If the demands of our modern world and the progressive
multiplication of stress and strain are to be met with a capacity
to sift and judge with healthy instinct, we must try to re-establish
a continuity with the past, based not on the empty shell or form
of tradition, but on a substance which has remained continuous
and recognizable despite its transformation into the incredible
shapes of today. What better example to illustrate the virtues of
real tradition than England, with its reassuring and stabilizing
framework of laws, customs and traditions, which have evolved
to maintain the truest democracy in the world?

[1] 26 October 1958.   1958

5. The Critics' Role

MUSIC is both subjective and rational by nature, reflecting both feeling and thought. Pure vibration is received or produced by the body while deliberately delaying or suspending outward action. In the concert hall the critic, along with the rest of the audience, is indeed the long-suffering target, and it is only fair that—on behalf of the audience and for personal reasons—he have some means, however silent and delayed, of retaliation.

The public performance is the focal point, the dead centre of the cyclone where, in the current jargon of our day, producer, middleman and consumer meet. But, unfortunately, how very wide of the mark this terminology falls! The producer (composer) is still one man at grips with himself, absolutely isolated and often uncertain of middleman (performer) or consumer (audience). The middleman, again, in solitary, concentrated effort, is in our case more concerned with understanding and identifying himself with the object than with its gift-wrapping—he does not want to get rid of it: he *is* it—he, like the composer, is giving himself. Finally the consumer, the public, we hope not equally solitary, but often consisting of a few dedicated souls, comes not to take something away under its arm, but to share a living experience, an experience in which composer, interpreter and audience are equally and immediately concerned.

The audience, however, is by nature passive—though it can inspire a performance by the quality, sincerity and sympathy of its listening—and, like a child, can only clap its hands frigidly or with fervour, or alternatively, boo.

The critic is therefore—as we hinted before—the spokesman both for and to the public on behalf of music, as the judiciary is both the will and the guide of society on behalf of justice and order. But what are justice and order in music today? The critic would not have reached his present eminence were he not

23

required by a mutiplying and generally open-minded public to define what is good and to explain why, giving his reasons.

In the past, not only deeds but also objects were clearly classified—they were good or bad, beautiful or ugly. Painters hardly ever painted ugly objects, except possibly some unprepossessing patron! Composers always returned beauty for all coin. At least the public knew where it was. First, as in African art, the sex of the artifact was left in no doubt. Nor was the public ever left in doubt in the past as to whether the object was rich or poor. Lovely brocades, sumptuous reds and royal purples, groaning tables, buxom ladies carried a clear message: truth, beauty and wealth enjoyed a not invariably holy alliance.

At least we could recognize ourselves or our ambitions, or even identify ourselves. With the exception of those realms of painting wherein the agony on the cross or some exquisitely introspective madonna depicted the troubled depths of life, music alone revealed, within its structures of sound and form, what was happening subjectively within the person. Music left us in no doubt as to what was happening within ourselves as the emotions were successively explored—reverence, prayer, pain, fear, pride, tenderness, love, humour, even hate or abhorrence. Until quite recently we could still recognize ourselves in a language entirely our own; but today we wonder who is to interpret and translate music and painting, which are one step further removed from the immediately recognizable—namely, no longer, first, what we see, or, second, what we feel, but what we *think* we know, or pretend to know; or what *he* (the composer) thinks—in a strange language, unknown to all but the composer himself.

Now words and thoughts have long been confused and are often assumed to amount to the same thing, although thinking is required before formulation in words can take place—that is, if we are not to utter mechanical automatic platitudes and pre-fabricated opinions. Words, however, are definitely not a prerequisite for thought, and particularly not for musical thought.

The use of words is a precious discipline which will refine and communicate; none the less the fabric of words is made of the words and thought, and the gold sovereign was still gold when buried as a nugget in some river-bed. Thought can remain wordless. In fact, the annals of art, war, crime and cooking bear ample witness to success as a result of thought as opposed to words, and even following *action* in defiance or in the absence of either thought or words. How many thoughtless actions were wordless too? 'Sometimes I sits and thinks and sometimes I just sits'— and today many an artist in his specialized way only thinks he thinks; he hardly seems even to sit, so as to avoid assuming any recognizable posture. You see where I am coming to—namely that we have perforce come to rely on those who at least can both sit and think at the same time. Only beware of words—though there is certainly less nonsense written about music than about painting; at least music itself takes so much time that it does not allow for as wordy a comment as painting—and, to our great advantage, its nature rules out simultaneous comment.

But although pure thought operates at the crystalline heights of pure mathematics and pure geometry, where presumably no further discussion is possible—at least not on basic premises—it is, as it were, the thoughts that artists are able to conjure or rather unable to abjure, that are fortunately sufficiently impure to allow of much discussion.

Surely in order to define a work of art or a process of thought we shall always have to establish (1) its organic unity; (2) its form, proportion and balance; (3) its inevitability in terms of its own canons; (4) its particular mixture of the recognizable and predictable with surprise and the unpredictable; (5) its expression of thoughts and visions, larger than and beyond man; (6) and last, but not least, a real living human impulse must, at least to my mind, infuse and justify the whole. In other words, it must be both universal and personal.

And so the new abstract, rational and irrational world of art should not escape the age-old fundamental criteria. The critic's role is indeed greater and more important than ever as new multitudes find music and painting and literature within their reach, and as they in turn exercise a choice and impart a bias and the test of immediacy to our art. These new multitudes do not bring any new or recognizable sense of style to their choice and taste—rather they show themselves curiously unprejudiced (open-minded, as I said before), and therefore crystallize their appreciation at two levels—the one satisfying unformed impulses, rude and raw (as in certain forms of jazz)—the other universal and perforce 'abstract'. In folk music, dance, sex, pride, and so forth were formalized so that form and content were one. Now content seems to be formless and form empty—or abstract, as you wish.

It is therefore all the more important for the critic to restore man to art. Despite our best efforts, by its very nature music can never be an abstraction, however thoughtful and objectless—for its object is the living man in time—nor can it be accidental, however improvised (as a monkey's, child's or lunatic's paintings, none of whom could compose without a given form or style), because improvisation is not the expression of accident but rather of the accumulated yearnings, dreams and wisdom of our very soul.

POSTSCRIPT: ON PROVIDING THE CADENZA

A music critic is quite right to deplore the lack of improvisatory élan in our contemporary virtuosi that is evident in the use of a 'standard cadenza'—itself incidentally a contradiction in terms. Until recently musical trends have been towards an increasing density and complexity. The growing precision of the composer's indications would seem to betray his profound distrust of the performer's every deviationary inclination. In fact, it demonstrates the development from a generally accepted and restricted style together with a regional ambience shared by composer, performer, and audience alike to the almost inconceivable complexity emanating from the ivory towers of composers of this century. So the performer, too, for the most part, is confined to interpreting a work and not to commenting on it in the form of free embellishment and improvisation. Indeed, these skills are still dominant in the classical Indian traditions as, on a lower level, in the jazz world, and there are encouraging signs of their resurgence among Western musicians of today—as with the American Lukas Foss and his group, to cite one example.

High standards in cadenzas set by such a great musician and violinist as Kreisler simply discourage those who feel incompetent to compose better ones. Even in the classical period Mozart and Beethoven distrusted the average performer, in many cases leaving their own cadenzas for posterity, while I need hardly plead the cause of such wonderfully integrated cadenzas as those of Mendelssohn, Elgar, Bartók, Bloch, or Shostakovitch for their violin concerti. Whether it is preferable to hear a personal cadenza rather than the best available one remains an open question. Certainly it would be better for the stimulation of the performer, but a possible hazard for the audience!

I myself have resorted to writing my own cadenzas wherever the available ones by Joachim, David etc., did not appeal to me (for example in Mozart Concerti, Nos. 1, 2, 4, and 5). The reason why I have not done the same for the Beethoven and Brahms concerti is because I have not felt confident so far of improving on Kreisler.

However, I differ from a certain music critic's opinion of the cadenza Kreisler wrote for the ending of the Larghetto of the Beethoven concerto: to my taste, far from 'preparing perfectly' for the Rondo, Kreisler, by introducing the six-eight rhythm of the finale prematurely, anticipating thereby what should only begin with its actual opening, and further using this rhythm chromatically when this is altogether out of keeping with the tenor of both Larghetto and Finale, weakens both the coda of the Larghetto and the fresh impact of the Finale.

As, to my way of thinking, it would be equally wrong to return to a Larghetto theme (as Joachim does) after the violent *fortissimo* shock of the full orchestra, I shelter behind Beethoven's own suggestion of 'cadenza ad libitum' and simply play an arpeggio to bridge the opening, two octaves apart, omitting all further musical comment as redundant, and closing the movement with Beethoven's own five solo notes. The Larghetto is already long enough and can stand by itself as one of the most exalted pieces of writing in the literature of the violin.

LONDON, 1962

6. The Violin

MAN'S PECULIAR PRIVILEGE is walking erect on two feet (and not on four): and thereby being forced to stretch his hands upwards to heaven. This conquering of gravity, space and height, as well as of horizon, is essential to violin-playing. This does not mean that we do not play with 'gravity' and put it to good use. Violin-playing, in fact all life, is a game between opposite, alternating principles, such as inhaling to fill the lungs and to contain space—and exhaling, or collapsing in passive relaxation.

In all physical activity technique depends upon use of space, so that the more expansion, extension or stretching we can develop, the better. We must never press a point to the bitter end, for if we do then we stop motion, unless, of course, we are compressing a spring for a rebound. We must never fly off the handle, for in doing so we dissipate strength. It is also important to allow an opposing force sufficient room to retrieve itself; otherwise the game is up. This is the principle of good sportsmanship. In holding an object between finger and thumb one creates a circle, and it is important to make that circle as round and large as possible in order to obtain the greatest amount of space within it. In other words, the more pressure we exert between, say, our two hands as we embrace something, the greater the space must be between that enclosure; we must stretch the two shoulders apart as we stretch the finger and thumb apart, making the circle larger. Space should increase with effort, not contract. Too often people have in mind a conception of control that is one of contraction, causing clenched hands and a restricted hold. This is absolutely wrong, both practically and philosophically.

Sickness and pain are forms of contraction—a folding back of the body and mind upon itself. It is as though the whole world had contracted into one's own focal centre, whether it be physical or mental. Love, on the other hand, is extension, a giving-out of oneself, an embracing of as wide a world as possible. Imagination is a stretching of horizons, as well as a deepening of conception. Activity and propulsion depend on repeated contractions of course, but between each of these a return, a reassertion of space, extension, and relaxation is essential. I wish to demonstrate, both literally and figuratively, that extension is positive and contraction negative, applying equally to love and hate, well-being and pain, assurance and nervousness, security and fear.

Conflicting and uncontrollable muscle tensions cause jerky, nervous movements, and at the same time are inhibiting or frustrating to the nervous system. This conflict of opposing muscles must be resolved, just as conflicting opinions must be resolved and placed in their proper perspective to prevent people quarrelling about them. Differences can only be resolved upon the basis of wider and broader terms of reference than either side commands singly.

If one wishes to understand topographical problems—the varied twists of the road or river, density of forest, and so on, the best way is literally to rise above them in a helicopter. In the same way, if we wish to find a resolution of opposing forces, we should cast the problem on to a higher and broader canvas, which will enable us to understand the relationship of these forces in the truer perspective of (historical) time and (geographical) space as well as of other factors in the cosmos.

This perspective can never be an absolute, but it can give a very good working approximation. It is possible to demonstrate this either philosophically or mathematically, for a 'true' perspective would be the zero point of action—absolute calm in the precise centre of time and space. I suppose we must agree that this perspective can only be hypothetical, for the most part. It is unattainable, except perhaps by a few mystic spirits through the ages, and lacks the warmth, compassion and prejudices of human life.

Life undoubtedly depends upon an irreducible minimum of bias and prejudice for continuance, these mutually destructive forces themselves being united in a greater motion. The circle, the cycle is the great 'resolver'. In the steam engine, the circle or wheel reconciles the piston's thrust and anti-thrust, and historical advancement may be compared to the steam engine's apparently inefficient progress.

The same applies to violin-playing. To play the violin it is necessary to form clear images of the interaction of four distinct directions, which parallel the four directions in the global circle. The four directions in violin-playing are: (a) and (b) horizontal push and pull; (c) carrying weight from above, and (d) supporting weight from below, which are the vertical directions. In the same way, bridges are built upon the opposing vertical principles of arch or suspension.

Each of these directions must be worked separately in each hand, each finger; on each place on the fingerboard and at each point of the bow; subsequently we put all in motion together. Each direction is worked in each position. Also, into each direction we build its opposition, creating regulated tension between the two, enabling us to support weight in motion and adjust speed in weight. Weight is carried into the very finger-tips and sustained upon flexible arcs, arches, circles and spirals.

The full use of every joint in the body—from the toes to the smallest end-joint of one's hands—is essential: from finger-tips' response to the ever larger joints of the wrist, elbow, shoulder, waist and the combined movement of all spinal vertebrae to hips and legs. These must move in one smooth flow, encountering nowhere a knot of resistance and finding everywhere just the right measure of support. Again, if this whole is not directed from the brain and heart, our voluntary and affective systems, then the motion is neither expressive nor useful. In fact, in teaching the violin I would begin with motion. Instead of concentrating on static positions (certainly not the first, which, lying at the far end of the fingerboard demands of an extended arm most carrying strength) I would first teach the basic motion of all, the horizontal swing of the whole body—which is propelled from each set of toes in turn and finds its next amplitude in the free swing of the upper extremities—shoulders, arms, hands, fingers. This is the whole motion and includes spine, hips, wrist, head, etc.

This motion should be learned with the arms at different rising levels, beginning with a hanging swing and building to a carrying (but equally free) swing. Finally, at a horizontal level we bend the left forearm vertically and the right horizontally, continuing the undulating swing, which is now prepared to receive the violin and bow. The first application of the bow on the violin should be elbow-pressure. Now we begin with the other end, i.e. the fingers of each hand, which we train in the balanced, flexible, tense yet springy hold of their respective instruments, violin and bow. These we teach by developing control, resistance, and speed in alternating our four basic directions with pressure and counter-pressure, weight and speed. These in turn are resolved into smaller or larger circles, or rather ellipses, as the horizontal is generally more demanding of space than the vertical.

Let us remember the three elements we use when playing: weight, balance and motion. Although we can be aware of them separately, we cannot really afford to separate them in practice.

If you study the motion of a wave along a whip, as you flick it, you will notice that the wave travels along the length of the whip from the point of impetus at a certain speed. This speed and amplitude is determined by the initial speed of the flick of the wrist, behind which must be (in order of precedence) the whole arm, the body, the legs. In other words, there is a delay, or rather a time-lag at every succeeding point as the wave of motion travels from the toes to the fingers, and back again. But do not hold the bow as you would a whip unless you can learn to handle the whip with flexible finger-tips!

Violin-playing is (a) a series of half-circles, embodying both the static principles of the arch, as in a bridge, and the dynamic principles of motion as exemplified by the pendulum; and (b) a series of whole circles, again embodying the static, structural, self-supporting principles of a sphere and the dynamic one of a wheel in motion.

These movements are both vertical and horizontal. Generally speaking, the vertical carry weight or support weight; the horizontal determine motion. They range from the smallest point to the largest. In the left hand the smallest circle or spiral is between the thumb and finger-tip, and this incorporates and 'absorbs' the fingerboard. Here again, as the downward pressure of finger on string is increased (by adding more weight) the upward pressure of the 'rub' of the thumb is equally increased, with the result that the circle between the two stretches in size and gains in stability. The same applies in the right hand between opposing fingers and bow-stick. Finally, both together. With both arms we form the largest, all-embracing circle, which encloses and absorbs, on different planes from horizontal to vertical, both the violin and the bow.

The other principal motion which we have already mentioned is the pendulum movement. This is used as a conservation of momentum. It is the simplest form of swinging movement, as in the left hanging elbow essential for vibrato change of positions. In the right arm-strokes again motion and gravity are at play in the balance of the head, as, of course, in the swing of the body as a whole.

There is no external support for the violinist as there is, for instance, for the 'cellist and the pianist. The violinist is self-contained and must be thoroughly self-reliant—self-supporting in fact. His right arm does not hang down freely from the shoulder, neither does his left arm fall into that more or less gentle curve it does when playing either the piano or the 'cello, a position which allows a natural swing as well as an easy blood circulation to infuse the motion of hands and fingers. The violinist must learn his pendulum-swinging motion with his arms and hands at a high level on different planes. He must do this without inhibiting the horizontal swing. That is why the near-horizontal movement of the hands on the fingerboard and on the bow must be studied deliberately, and, except in the very rarest of cases, it just does not come naturally to the violinist. This is the chief reason why good violin-playing and teaching are less common than with other instruments.

Of all instrumentalists, he must really learn to catch a motion on the wing, to perpetuate impetus, and gather momentum, finding nowhere and indeed not allowing any static support. From the very beginning he must learn to float and carry; to drift with the stream of motion or emotion. He must be able to set a motion going and subtly to push it along, as he does, interpretatively, the rhythmic pulse of a piece.

Motion is the very life-blood of a violinist—he has no instrument to rest on; his stance must be erect, yet supple, so that like a graceful reed he may wave with the breeze and yet have his head firmly supported in a line through the spine to the feet.

He is a conservationist, for he conserves motion, precious motion, minutest motion. Not for him the somewhat exhibitionist and fiery springing from seat or keyboard of a virtuoso pianist, or the erratic acrobatics of some conductors. The violinist is confined to his instrument: the distance his fingers and hands can travel is severely limited, and the bow can only leave the string under precise, controlled conditions. In fact the only ways that a violinist can escape, or rather indulge in excess motion, are by hip-swaying or rolling from one leg to another (a motion which should be reduced as far as possible to the purely horizontal) or excessive movement of his head, and perhaps least disturbing or distracting to the onlooker, his toes!

I have spoken of motion, of the static strength and dynamic movement of arcs, arches and circles, but have not explained the point of rest. As I said, the cellist and pianist find their points of support or rest on their instruments and on their chairs, as well as in a direct hanging-down of the arms from the shoulders; the violinist makes his own. Rest is not floating without direction; it is either a hanging *down* or a finding support from below— abandoning oneself completely to *one* exclusive supporting source. We rest when we are drawn irresistibly to one centre and find security by being supported by it.

When our arms and hands are allowed to drop freely from our shoulders, they rest. But when we play the violin, we must build our own system of suspension and support; we cannot relax the whole limb at any one moment, but we relax one part while supporting with the other.

The simplest form of joining motion and rest, as I have said, is the pendulum, which is supported at one end yet has motion at the other. In the same way, we must find alternative support for each and every left-hand finger-to-thumb spiral (or near circle) on the fingerboard, and we must allow even this support a full measure of wide oscillation, still allowing the elbow to hang and move as a pendulum. The opposite effect (for example, in the metronome) takes place when we support the elbow, keeping the hand high above, hanging over the fingerboard, to which support is transmitted by the thumb, allowing the hand or fingers to 'pend' invertedly. These two forms of pendulum motion are essential to vibrato, change of position and finger-fall.

The same holds true for the right hand, where a combination of fingers creates circles or spirals with the thumb; as between thumb and second finger, thumb and first or indeed thumb and third and fourth fingers. And arches are created between the fingers themselves, as between first and third or first and fourth, or first with or against third and fourth. All such circles and arcs must be as spatially full and round as possible, and in constant adjustment; these the right hand carries or leans on, varying in minutest degrees between the two extremes of weight, applied and suspended. The bow and fingers are almost constantly in motion, while the elbow and shoulder both propel and rest upon the finger and wrist-arches, or support the hanging wrist and fingers.

To those of us who have to change from one habit to another (I hope from a worse one to a better one) I would like to say a word about the means of doing it. Between the two habits must come a point of zero tension, which is pure balance without effort. You cannot go from a wrong strength to a right strength without going through a period of 'no strength'. In other words, if you are already exerting strength in the wrong way, and exert more strength to try and break that habit, then you will only dig yourself deeper into the bad habit. Until you can first dissolve the wrong tension, the wrong grasp, and bring about absolute flexibility and suppleness in your point of contact, you will never build a new habit successfully.

The secret of technique lies in finding these extreme points and positions in the correct form, and filling in between them an infinite number of degrees. Every point of rest, like every motion, must be understood in both its vertical and horizontal implications. Above all, the secret of technique is evenness; the evenness of stresses, or rather, the balance between counteracting tensions, pulling in opposite directions. This balance enables the fingers, and, therefore, the notes themselves, to be formed in absolute, even succession. It is evenness of pressure, of volume, that enables us to achieve control, and from this control comes our 'interpretation', which, as I explain in the next chapter, may be regarded as a very discreet and refined form of distortion. These are the two elements required for successful playing: the technical one, which achieves evenness, and the interpretative one, which demands an awareness of the uneven, the unpredictable, and the slightly distorted.

DARTINGTON, 1962

7. *Improvisation and Interpretation*

FOR ALL MUSICIANS, for all those people whose lives are music, I have the greatest admiration and respect. My life is made up on the one hand of flying all over the world and dealing with many different aspects of music, while on the other I lead a very solitary and confined life, by reason of my being principally a soloist. This life is entirely different from the gregarious musical activity in classroom and orchestra, which is so exacting in its detail of organization and so demanding of steady unglamorous virtue.

Improvisation, you may think, is something which is far removed from the routine of teaching and playing, but I will try and show you that it is, in fact, very intimately associated with routine; and that the one could hardly exist without the other.

Improvisation is an essential element in all art. In music we are apt to assume that the nomadic gipsy musicians embody the purest form of improvisation in their playing. We think this because they play without a printed score and have probably never even been 'taught' the particular instrument on which they play. But we should consider too the Indian classical musicians, who are not nomadic, yet who weave their own magic spell and who are highly cultivated and extremely disciplined musicians. Their improvisations are more rational, analytic, and complex than those of the gipsy musicians, who are more nostalgic, passionate and abandoned.

We also have the improvisation of the African jazz musicians, who illustrate, like the gipsies, the phenomenon of spontaneous combustion, and whose improvisations arise from an almost visceral compulsion. It is, as it were, a return to blind emotion, powerful and contagious in the extreme, but not cerebrally structured in the manner of Indian classical music.

Then there is the Western musical tradition, to which we belong, and this I would liken to a two-stage rocket, in that it requires two separate efforts to bring about its achievement. These are: (a) the composer's effort, in which aim, direction, style and form are implicit, and (b) the interpreter's, on which the composer's effort depends before his 'message' can attain its point of impact, its destination.

This separation of functions is, of course, typical of the growing complexity of our contemporary life, with its differentiation and specialization of functions. But it would be a great mistake to assume that because the Western musician is performing a piece already written, the element of improvisation is absent. Just the opposite, in fact. Improvisation is of exquisite subtlety, although, I will admit, often elusive; but if it were absent then I am certain that our music would cease to hold in its power those who have surrendered themselves to it. There is admittedly a great difference in degree between the creative improvisation of the composer and the creative improvisation of the performer, but if this element of improvisation is absent in the interpretation the performance has no communicative power.

I would like, at this point, to explain my theory of 'distortion' as it applies to the musician interpreting the works of a composer. 'Distortion' is, perhaps, an unhappy word, but I will explain the sense in which I use it. It is the manifestation of the spontaneous, the immediate and impulsive forces of music, as of life. For example, we may have a calm lake with no wind, no ripple— and no distortion. But with the coming of a breeze upon the waters a multitude of unique ephemeral events take place which owe nothing, as it were, to past or future but which are instantaneous reactions reflecting the very moment, a rounded, wellnigh complete action of creation, because it is bounded at both ends, before and after, with oblivion, and spatially with apparent irrelevance.

It is interesting that we, as human beings, feel this reaction, interpret this reaction to the immediate as the expression of spontaneity. A large part of our existence must of course conform to established patterns, which ignore the immediate.

Dangerous as it is to lead a life bereft of ordering principles and entirely at the mercy of fleeting reactions, these minute sympathetic vibrations engendered by the breeze become essential in any creative or recreative process. For they reflect continuous change, which is in fact life in creation.

My theory of distortion arises from this unpredictable succession of unique events or spontaneous sympathetic reactions which are of the instant. The opposite of all this is a levelling, a submitting of ourselves to routine and habit. Art then becomes an exciting adventure, the more so in fact as the basic form and structure of our life and recreation is strong and sound. Therefore let us not despise this structure, for we need the mechanical in order to gain control and develop continuity. Without it we could not possibly express ourselves freely. It is essential that the major part of our technique should be under the control of automatic habits. Having achieved this control then our interpretative power can be allowed freedom to express itself to the full extent of its imagination. Conversely, to achieve this technique we must feel inspired so that we may submit to its disciplines with good grace. We see, therefore, that there is an inter-action between these two seemingly contradictory yet complementary conditions.

Distortion can only be measured against a fixed standard, especially when we are playing that subtlest of instruments, the violin, for then we require the smallest perceptible distortion, and it is important for us to be able to judge the exact measure of the deviation. To do this, we must eliminate all impurities of un-evenness and basic tensions unrelated to the particular work we are interpreting, in order to allow the violin to reflect the purest, the most delicate oscillations. These vital oscillations are a kind of radar, turned outward as well as inwards so that it can reflect both the momentary and the universal. Not only with music, of course, but with all art, with all life, we begin by stretching out in two seemingly opposite directions, but ultimately we complete a circle in which the momentary and the timeless become one. If you like, the individual can see his relationship with infinity.

We know that in the lives of certain composers such as Bach, Beethoven and, more recently, Bartók, early immature passions gave way to an extraordinary serenity in later years. Serenity suggests a completion of the circle, of this relationship with infinity. It is the reconciliation of the two opposite directions.

There are, of necessity, basic rules and forms for every art, and against these the artist must measure his impulses, his passions, his inspirations. We can call this 'extra' by different names, but what we mean is that vitalizing spark which is no longer hands, heart, brains or even a particular moment, but a cohesion of all these, and more.

I would now like to investigate the basic rules we have been discussing in relation to the deviationary, or improvisational.

There is a rhythmic pulse in every variety of relationship contained in our accepted rules, on which we base our discipline of form. There is the simple one to one, one to two, and so on, but it all boils down to a difference in speeds and amplitudes. The harmonic relationship between notes is only a more rapid succession of pulses than what is usually recognized as rhythm. It is actually only rhythm in top gear, as it were. When these relationships are slow enough for our rational mind to perceive, we recognize what we call rhythm, but when they become much faster, too fast for rational perception as individual percussive units, then we have continuous sound.

Now this second stage of the rhythmic impulse takes its form in particular notes of definite pitch, in the formulation of a scale. In this respect, every civilization has tried to put together a few sounds which would form some sort of continuity having some affinity to each other. This relationship is both one of proportion and one of proximity. Proportion is the basis of measurement whereas proximity is the melodic element in which one note leans on another or provides the embellishment or ornamentation of one note by others.

I have tried to reduce the three elements of rhythm, harmony, and melody to their basic origin to show their position in relation to each other. Now these may seem mere abstractions, but they become practical as the musician disciplines himself to obey implicitly and automatically the dictates of a particular rhythm in a particular sequence of notes. In all his disciplinary efforts, evenness and predictability are the watchwords, in spite of the fact that these disciplines may vary according to particular style or tradition. In gipsy music these disciplines are relatively simple because the music is mainly melodic; using only two scales and remaining harmonically simple. The gipsies are deeply involved emotionally and have little time for abstract inventions or constructions. They are a nomadic people and their 'baggage' is light.

African music is powerfully rhythmic and percussive; being, as it were, incendiary by nature. One cannot imagine either a gipsy or an African spending six hours a day practising. Now the Indian classical musician practises perhaps more than any other musician, for he has to master an elaborate and complex system of both rhythm and melody. Although there are vast numbers of formalized scales, vast numbers of melodic embellishments, vast numbers of rhythmic involutions of unparalleled complexity to be mastered, yet all the while the musician must retain his original inspirational fire. It is no wonder that the ultimate atmosphere created by this Indian music appeals in a large measure to the intellect. It is liberating to the spirit and conducive to meditation and to an awakening of the sense of the universal and infinite.

Finally in our own western music, rhythm and melody are less complex, less formalized and stylized than in Indian classical music. There is, however, a third element in music; that of harmony and/or dissonance.

All these elements proved too much for one performer's improvisation so, finally, the composer came to compose the whole piece, which, when completed, the performer inherited. So we have a division of labour, and this division led to the performer's concentrating much more on the *means* of playing. It was after this division between composer and interpreter, that the latter became specifically a singer, a violinist, a pianist, etc., in other words a mere instrument. He then fell into the danger of forgetting his primary purpose, that of *creating* music, and thereby sterilized his own birthright to re-creation.

But let us look for a moment at the need for technical accomplishment. Of course, we must be accomplished, technically; and we must be able to apprehend and control musical forms. We must make all these disparate elements (of unequal length and strength) equal in strength and flexibility, just as we have to train our disparate fingers. By these means alone we are able to release the unique, peculiar quality of each and every note.

Judging by common denominators rather than by uncommon and infinitely variable differentiation, we say that to the Africans all white people look the same; all communists look alike to all capitalists, and vice versa. It is the same with notes on the printed page. We see a great many notes divided into arbitrary values;

four to a beat, eight to a beat, and so on, and, of course, it is important to be able to distinguish and play them as they are printed, evenly and correctly; but the vital impulse in each note of a composition may be compared with that 'divine spark' in every human being, not visible to the human eye. And this is another matter altogether. Take as a specific example the first two solo bars of the Beethoven Violin Concerto.

First of all, they are, as a group, the inversion of the two preceding bars, which are themselves preceded by units of one and two bars:

Two groups of four descending bars are answered by the violin with two groups of four ascending bars. Here is the first ascending chord in the piece covering these two octave ranges: there has been a preceding broken chord descending, towards the very beginning, before the first *fortissimo* in the opening *tutti*:

—again in groups of two bars, four notes plus four.

The following double *forte* represents a span of one octave, but is only one bar long:

The solo entry is the first example of that particular form ascending over two bars.

Already we understand that it is more than just an arpeggio, it is something relating to the whole work. Equally important is the rhythmic element. For example these four opening notes, the drum beats which constitute the basic pulse of the first movement, see the first solo bars come halfway to being a melodic figure. It is not *quite* melodic, for the notes bear no unique, independent nor particular relation to each other. It is not purely rhythmic either, not as for instance the opening bar of the timpani part. It is already more melodic than the opening timpani beats. Although retaining something of the strictness of the opening bars, it *must* at the same time have a soaring quality.

This first entry of the violin also has an interesting span. It goes from the A to the G: and that is the very core of the opening phrase of the concerto, which is:

achieved by melodic contiguous motion as opposed to the disjoined motion of the broken chord—and as if to stress its perivation the solo violin continues with:

which is the opening melody, the sequel to the first four notes above.

Thus these eight notes acquire more and more meaning as we think about them in relation to this particular work. We can develop this investigation further, and the more we do so, the more we see that these notes couldn't be any others. For instance, the relation in Beethoven's music between the scale and the broken chord is very close. In the slow movement of this concerto, Beethoven takes out the intervening notes, leaving a broken chord pure and simple:

which in the first movement is:

It is the same figure, but it has now become an arpeggio; a broken chord. I think this shows that throughout the work there is a relationship between the scale and the broken chord.

But how do we use this relationship? We have already discovered that the span is from A to the G, and it covers the two octaves because the two octaves have been covered on the way down and therefore it has to rise at least that much. Beethoven adds yet another octave in the form of a grace note.

The grace note provides the impulse, a surprising sort of spring, as if you prepared to put your foot down before actually doing so. The octave also belongs organically to the piece, as it comes first

then

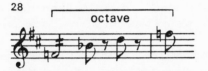

then as we saw

Therefore the violin begins with the spanning of an octave, which, when the violin finally gets to the solo melody becomes

and is the answer to the preceding octave scale on the dominant.

Let us now consider the three stages in the interpretation. First, the exaggeration of all possible distortions; second, the reduction of these; and finally the third stage when we need to completely digest and assimilate all deviations. We must aim to play a passage so that it may appear even, and yet retain enough of the original distortion for the vital element to be recognized, allowing for the interpretation to vary slightly each time. The variations in interpretation are infinite, but they must always be within the context of the piece; within the justification that the relationship of the notes allows.

We know for one thing that the C sharp and the E in this bar are less important than the A and G. We must try to connect the A to the G, arching over the two intervening notes. By holding the A, hurrying the C sharp and E and accenting the G—by playing the two middle notes less strongly, yet making a crescendo to the G—and by continually counter-checking these distortions against the essential basic pulse, we finally produce a living image, an even rise of great dignity; this is freedom versus law.

We have now established certain relationships between the notes in terms of time and volume. To play them perfectly naturally you need to have either an unspoiled instinct or that combination of instinct with analytical procedure which serves as both an inspiration and a check. The inspiration is wonderful because it bears you along on the obviously organic and inevitable flow of a composition, while at the same time it holds you in check. The subtle but radical relationships of elements must be held in balance, and no one element allowed to disrupt the overall pattern.

Finally, returning to our example, perhaps the chief element to be conveyed is the whole aura of these notes: expectation, dignity, direction; a sense of forward motion which must always bear relation to the first timpani bar. Thus expression must not burst the bonds of measure, nor must measure stifle expression.

Such is the element of improvisation in classical Western music, in music that is already composed, already written. It is obvious that the Indian musician improvises, but it isn't always as obvious that the Western musician also improvises, although, of course, he does so to a lesser degree.

The rules of Indian music are so very formal and elaborate that they provide nearly as much guidance and often allow as little freedom as the written score of the Western composer. The elements of law and freedom must both exist, and no one, Indian, African or Western, can improvise in a void. We must all have guiding lines. Very often the Western musician, especially when he has been playing for many hours in orchestras with one eye on the score and the other on the conductor, loses all sense of this essential element of improvisation as it applies to him. However, he is always ready to sense it, to feel it, otherwise he wouldn't be a musician in the first place. It is good, therefore, to remind him that this improvisatory element is as important in our music as in all other music, whether the most primitive African or the most elaborate Indian.

The contemporary trend is towards the breaking down of all barriers, and there is an enormous mixing of influences, of strains, of styles from all over the world. In the United States, the mixing between the African and the European has already happened. There has been a fusion between the percussive rhythm and the tonic-dominant harmony, which was the original, rather simple form of jazz. But today we have more than just these two elements. We have, for instance, the Indian influence and cross-fertilization; a sharp stimulus, which is already producing improvisation in every shape and form. Improvisation has become the order of the day, often at the simplest level of natural, accidental, and primitive expression. People get together and make sounds which may or may not have shape, but which at the least are productive for the performer, if not for the listener. The result may not be a work of art, but it is, none the less, a wonderful release from the humdrum routine of everyday life. Imagine young housewives being able to bang away at a pot as hard as they like, instead of always washing or watching it anxiously. This improvisation provides an emotional release— something the world sorely needs—but it is not until it has undergone the formal disciplines we have been discussing that it can become a work of art. The differences between the 'classical' musicians who are tied to the metronome and those who let their hair grow long and play as the spirit moves them are gradually disappearing.

I strongly approve of this development, which is restoring the essential, vital element in music. This trend, due to both young and old alike, enhances the delight of making music oneself, independent of mechanical means.

We have so much to learn from the improvisation of other musical styles that if I were to generalize on the contemporary trend I think I would say that it is the desire to capture the ecstatic quality of life; to catch it on the wing before it falls. Perhaps the musician is particularly fortunate in this respect because his life, the rhythm of his existence, is dependent on laws which are so often forgotten in the synthetic existence that many people must lead in a factory or office. The musician is still receptive to the vibrations that reach him, and he is able to communicate them. Perhaps it is because of this that he is also aware, consciously or unconsciously, that there is proportion in nature; that there is the soaring glory of freedom and there is also the price of freedom; of which he perhaps more than anyone else is fully cognizant. The price of freedom for all musicians, both composers and interpreters, is tremendous control, discipline and patience; but perhaps not only for musicians. Do we not all find freedom to improvise, in all art, in all life, along the guiding lines of discipline?

LONDON, 1963

8. Radio and Recording

MY MUSICAL LIFE began in that prolonged twilight (or should I say twi-sound?) before the day of radio, when the genuine silence of night was yet unbroken by the amplified horrors of 'Silent Night' carolling the season's blessings. It is difficult for me to realize—no doubt because it is unpalatable— that my present words mark a major anniversary of BBC Sound Transmission.[1]

Well do I remember the awesome intrusion into our childhood home in San Francisco of that first crystal receiver which, like some spoilt dog, could only respond to patient coaxing with most uncrystal-like whines, groans and grunts. But then I have no excuse for making fun of radio's first efforts, considering that my own sounds about that time were nothing to brag about. By the time I was ready to play half-way decently, radio was more than ready for me.

The very first time I broadcast, with Walter Damrosch conducting the New York Symphony, I was about fourteen. As I was playing the *Symphonie Espagnole* by Lalo, it was no doubt also intended as an edifying occasion when 'great and serious' music is provided for a presumably recalcitrant public merely for the charitable purpose of giving material encouragement to poor musicians. Whether unique or edifying, however, this occasion was powerless to alter my mother's stringent timetable of convalescent treatment, which was intended to break a cold I had nursed all the way from Genoa on the S.S. *Conte di Savoia*. Indeed, the two mustard plasters, applied both fore and aft, with which I sallied forth to meet this new challenge were the conditions, *sine qua non*, of my keeping this engagement. Fortunately I did not

[1] This talk was given in 1949 on the occasion of the 25th anniversary of the BBC.

47

lose my skin in this new venture—no doubt I was the first Redskin
to emerge unscathed in New York City in several centuries—and
I can recall countless subsequent delightful broadcasts in all the
capital cities of the world, when I had nothing else to suffer but
playing the violin.

Of all these occasions, the most satisfying, memorable and
numerous were those I did with the BBC from London, during
the war, from Bedford, or from other parts of Great Britain, or
the Commonwealth. This is because, of all broadcasting services
all over the world, far and away the most enlightened, the most
consistently high in quality of programmes, performances and
receptions are those of the BBC.

Free of that condescending pretension to educate the reluctant
masses, the *illiterate* (as if the illuminating and beautiful were for
ever the antithesis of the pleasurable and useful), and although a
quasi-official institution, with neither dogmatic nor commercial
bias, avoiding the cheap and easy devices of arresting maximum
attention by methods both fair and foul, it has provided a civilized
diet of the best information, the broadest range of music, literature
and thought of all densities from lightest to heaviest. This it has
done longer and better than any other service in the world. As a
member of the BBC Music Advisory Committee I am ceaselessly
impressed with the pertinent choice of works arrived at by the
staff, with full recognition of the various requirements of (a)
timeless values of all periods; (b) fashion and curiosity and (c)
contemporary fact—and fancy.

Indeed, as perhaps never before, sound broadcasting is liberated
to roam and explore the vast regions of man's thought and
imagination, while the miraculous medium of sight-transmission
has, by its very nature, communicated largely the instantaneous,
brash and sensational, leaving its less flashy and less dramatic
antecedent a more homogeneous and integrated field of
endeavour.

In the field of television, too, the BBC has led all other services.
Indeed, today it represents an overpowering demand for a new
dimension of art and intellect in millions of homes throughout
the realm, which is both the by-product of the years of good fare
hitherto provided and the cause for expanded efforts on the part
of the BBC to meet the high standards required and exacted by

the best informed, least prejudiced, most artistically sensitive and
awakened audiences in this wide but shrinking world.

As a member of the public I have the feeling that of all
institutions the BBC belongs to me and not to any particular
power-group, either dogmatic or commercial, and as a human
being who has in all facets of life, musical and otherwise,
collaborated ever more closely and actively with this admirable
institution, I take particular pride in marking this anniversary
milestone in the most distinguished history in the twentieth-
century fabric of communications.

It is a comment upon our times that the new science of sound
recording[1] has had an enormous impact on the art of playing the
violin, that most perfect of all instruments.

For how many millennia did man wait for the mirror (although
there were to be found lakes in which the unfocused image could
be reflected, as our voices can be thrown back from rocky cliffs
with elusive echo), and now, although we *can* hear ourselves, it
is with an effort that we do so objectively, as anyone who listens
to his own recorded speaking voice for the first time can well
judge. It is only with the gramophone that self-criticism, and I
may add, audience criticism, has reached its present high standard.

Undeniably this has made for better, more accurate, cleaner
performances, and has helped violinists and other string players
to play more in tune. Casals once told me in utter earnestness
that before Ysaÿe no violinist played in tune! I find this difficult
to believe, for it seems inconceivable that Paganini, Spohr,
Vieuxtemps, Joachim and the rest could have been consistently
out of tune without noticing it. Yet before the era of the repeatable performance (almost a contradiction in terms), there was no
opportunity for the ear to form a sound judgement as to the
authoritative interpretation; it could only decide at each performance what seemed right at that particular moment. Moreover, the
qualities which make for a satisfying performance and those which
make for a satisfying recording are not always identical, just as
the studio portrait and the candid photograph are not identical.
Theoretically these qualities are never incompatible, but in practice the impact of the performer's personality or of the recreated

[1] This section is from an article provided for the twenty-fifth anniversary of
the International Federation of the Phonographic Industry.

emotion may occasionally eclipse minor defects. These latter may seriously mar the pleasure of even the greatest performance when turned on with a switch for the hundredth time behind the performer's back! The converse is equally true, and a perfect performance, the smallest detail of which is established and predictable, can become as dull and even as unbearable as a tinted family portrait with its frozen smiles.

Some so-called primitive people have a superstition about the photograph, and are now no doubt evolving one about the sound recording. They feel that with each click of the camera, with each photograph taken, a distinct portion of the life and vitality of the subject is destroyed. What they feel is perhaps a basic antithesis between their unpredictable life and the predictable recording. A recording tends to cast such people into self-conscious attitudes and poses, which inhibit their free expression. If this is so, or even only partly so, then the opposite is also true. Does our contemporary phenomenon of massive mechanical reproduction of every conceivable act and thought reflect our standardization, and the abysmal dearth of inspiration and instinct in millions of people geared to the mechanical age? Or is it a phenomenon related to a terrifying lack of feeling, and to a fanaticism lacking in humility, and so deliberately stifling compassion? It is an age-old trait peculiar to man that his rational and God-imitating nature has tried to impose a wretched pattern on life at all stages of his ignorance.

This is one of the drawbacks of a favourite recorded performance—it tends to crystallize an act which should always retain some fluidity. Today, when the music-lover can hear a dozen different performances of a chosen work, this hazard is lessened, but, none the less, persists. I would like to warn the record enthusiast not to play a beloved work too often, for this may ultimately destroy its magic. I would also like to encourage the amateur music-maker to play an instrument, a real musical instrument, not merely the gramophone. No, not even a stereo-gramophone that can blast the four walls asunder with a dozen loudspeakers and paralyse all the dogs in the neighbourhood with too true fidelity and upper partials. Better far to play a real instrument on which you can really *make* music, with all the risks of failure, wrong notes and horrid sounds.

In parentheses, I wish there were a series of recordings to teach counterpoint, harmony and the figured bass. With only four loud-speakers Bach and Bartók counterpoint would emerge with unbelievable chiselled clarity. Those fundamental principles governing voice-line, imitation, dominant and subsidiary motives, and the relative importance of notes (melodically, harmonically and rhythmically), would be easy to demonstrate to the listener. Such a device might, who knows, bring about a re-birth of the amateur composer. Music and composition require a firm basis in 'the people' in order to produce their finest flowers; just as poetry and drama belonged to the people in medieval and Elizabethan times, and gave rise to a flowering that England still enjoys.

To return to recording techniques, it is certainly important that the recording crew, apart from possessing technical knowledge, should be sensitive and sympathetic listeners. I am grateful to the English crews in London who have the capacity of combining factual precision and discipline with poetic insight in the highest degree.

Already in the brief but brilliant history of recording science it is possible to discern changes in fashion and interpretation, as in the somewhat older sister-technique of photography. The rise of recording has been all the more brilliant and amazing in that, unlike the visual arts, it has had no recourse to tangible paintings and objects as a basis for comparison and critique. I can foresee the time when scholars bent upon historical research will study the trends of styles in the recordings of the past just as they study the wimples, farthingales and liripipes of other centuries.

It is difficult to know whether to be pleased or sad that in the future our own present performances will no longer enjoy the aura of mystery that those of, say, Chopin or Tartini now command. However, in the name of progress I congratulate this great industry on its Silver Jubilee. Speaking as a violinist may I add, in a timid voice, the prayer that the next generation limit its rate of progress from the spectacular and the explosive to one more in step with the slow and painful progress of the practical musician.

LONDON, 1949

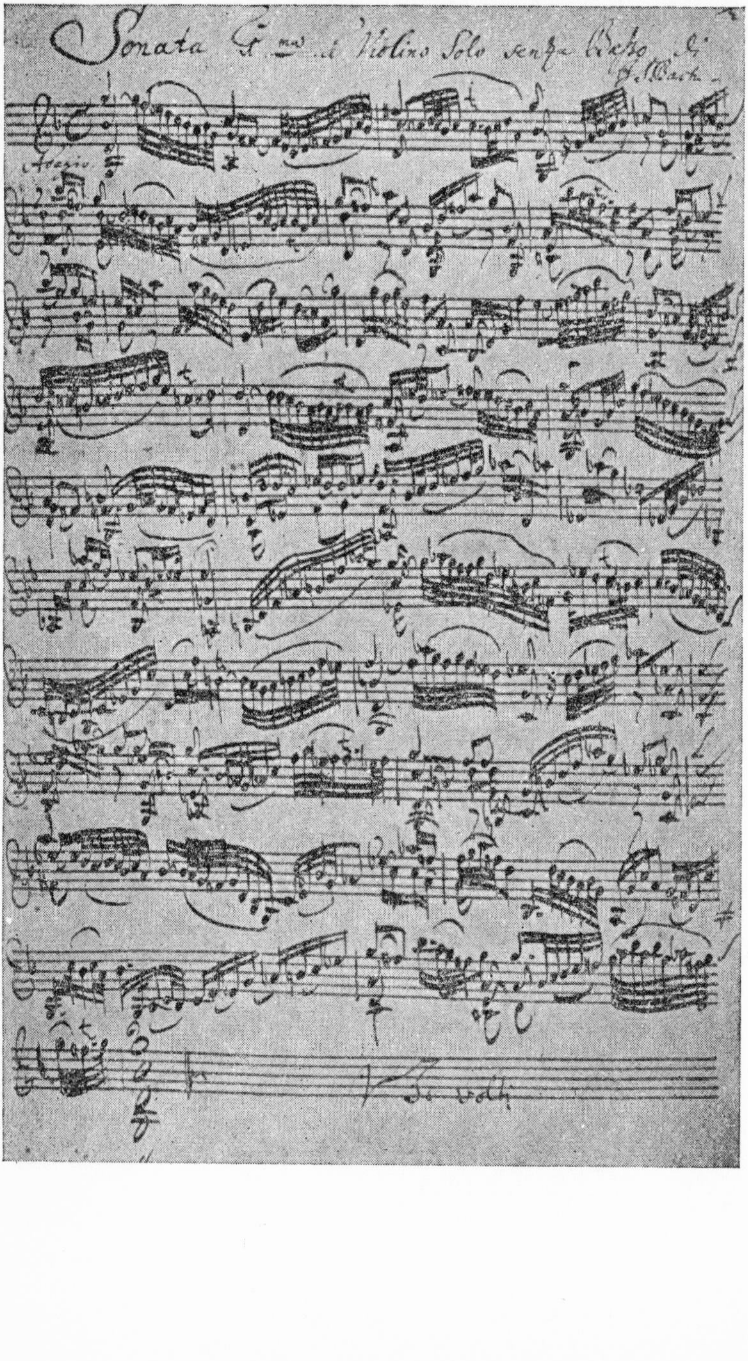
Sonata 1ma à Violino Solo senza Basso di
J. S. Bach
Adagio

9. Three Great Composers

BACH, BEETHOVEN, BARTÓK

LOOKING AT BACH'S AUTOGRAPH,[1] I seem to see a heavenly body in motion and to witness, as it were, the unfolding of a natural phenomenon according to the immutable law of which man himself is but a fraction. No wonder we feel Bach's music to be universal.

And again, look at the strong inevitable flow of his handwriting, as of a river implacably moving towards the sea and yet infinitely pliable and flexible, accommodating itself to every stone, hill or mountain and to every smallest obstacle in its path.

His work can be compared with the germination of a seed, of which the ensuing plant is predetermined in every minutest detail of shape and function, and by the same token is entirely bound up with its environment of light, air and food.

The conception in Bach's music is of the broadest. Just as some people conceive of a room in a house, and others of a house in a city, and still others of the city as part of a country, the country part of the world and the world part of the universe—so there is always in Bach's music a conception which transcends the individual work. For instance, the sonatas for solo violins are conceived in the six best keys for the instrument, in that they have a minimum of accidentals, and they proceed in a very logical order: G minor, B minor, A minor, D minor, C major, E major. The two keys which have the least number of open strings are used for the two partitas where there is a minimum of polyphonic writing: the E major and the B minor. The biggest fugues are the C major and the A minor, keys without any accidentals at all. Another example is the great polyphony of the Chaconne in D minor (only one accidental), and the arrival of

[1] See facing page.

the major chord at exactly the half-way point in the composition, as a matter of fact four bars before the two-voice section in the major. This shows that even while composing Bach knew both consciously and instinctively exactly where he was according to an all-embracing plan, often larger than the work itself.

As there is a timeless quality to his music and thus also to his hand, which is but the automatic reflection of his impulses, there is also a universally present quality—a candid, instantaneous quality which is more than a photographic flash, because unlike a photograph or a painting it exists in extended time and space simultaneously. As a painting is an ideal organization of space, so is this handwriting, in its own way, an ideal organization of time. (Note also the extraordinary way in which the available paper-space is organized.) It is not the performing time alone, however, but the creative time that I mean, although in Bach's case, as in Mozart's, the two come near to being the same. See with what clarity, independence and yet submissiveness each voice is led and portrayed.

Why have all subsequent editions abandoned Bach's notation? This habit betrays the progressive degeneration of the independent contrapuntal line into the harmonic cluster. It betrays the gradual transition from the horizontal to the vertical, a transition characteristic of all society and reflected in music, architecture, and in fact all the arts. It is the evolution from the individual to the mass, and also from a smooth and melodic continuity, like that of heredity, to the transitional, arbitrary, jagged and expendable qualities of our modern environment.

Why can we not respect the aesthetic system which enables one to see and to follow each voice and to treat it linearly as the independent entity it is? How vulgar an attitude we betray by printing this music harmonically only, instead of contrapuntally as well.

We have noted the paradox of the apparent conflict and actual equilibrium of opposing elements, as in the simultaneous independence and submission of each voice (independence born of the eternity of each part and submission born of membership of a greater unit). Let us now examine further paradoxical revelations—of great strength without brutality, of sentiment without sentimentality, of reasoned ecstasy or sober intoxication. The impassioned expression of this music and of this handwriting is conveyed through a touching simplicity, as for instance in the sounds of a flute or an oboe. The extravagance of emotion and pro-fundity of meditation is clothed with the greatest economy—and the immeasurable and the infinite is transmitted in form and even measure. The fabric of dreams is vested in architecture, and the history of mankind in melody. To us musicians, Bach is our own flesh and blood as meaningfully as are the sacraments to a Christian.

Whereas, for instance, Beethoven discovered and understood his fellow-men through his own emotions, and we recognize ourselves in him, Bach discovered himself through mankind, or through an emotion larger than himself, and therefore mankind recognizes in Bach's music something greater than itself. Perhaps one can say that Beethoven, Schumann and the other Romantics each expressed their own flesh and blood. Bach is one stage removed from this kind of expression, and is to that extent symbolic in the same way as his Lord.

We return to Bach as to a greater church, as to a musical Christ. Although musical sound is intangible and so presumed to be incorruptible, Bach's music is not impervious to misinterpretation, any more than Jesus's words. Subsequent generations have not always matched their actions to the 'Word'. As all humanity's most noble achievements are reduced to the limitations of the eyes, the ears, the minds and the hearts that apprehend them, so has Bach's music too been often distorted by passing fashions. Blame also the unhappy human habit which obliges people to distort a universal principle to a particular end.

Fortunately we have in Bach's handwriting tangible evidence of his will and his emotion, and we can for ever be reminded of and be recalled to the very letter and the spirit of his sermons.

GSTAAD, 1957

No composer has ever refined his raw material to the degree of purity that BEETHOVEN achieved. Wrestling with it until he transformed it into concentrated statements of intense meaning, he focused his fire in the process. So often today, when composers begin with a raw material already in an advanced state of abstraction, there can be no such physiological and emotional process, no process of distillation or even of decay, no self-immolation in the creative achievement of conversion.

Beethoven's achievement is an extraordinary universality of utterance, a universality partaking alike of the truth of a mathematical equation and of the truth of a universal human experience.

Violinists must remain for ever grateful that Beethoven composed at a time when string instruments, and particularly the violin, were still dominant, when the perfect (or nearly perfect) fifth ruled the harmonic world, when singable melody was still an essential element of music, and before harmonic and chromatic density, or the sheer mass and volume of the newly developing piano, or the effects of our tremendous orchestras nearly overwhelmed the single violin.

So it is that Beethoven gave the violin a greater meaning and depth of expression than it had ever known before, in one way almost turning it into the literary instrument that is the piano. His violin writing is a deeply moving intellectual discourse, more a language than a poem, ennobling and thought-provoking rather than purely pleasure-giving. I would say for instance that we listen to Mozart, but that we concentrate on Beethoven.

In spinning these seamless and endless phrases beyond the range and potential of any voice, in exacting a clarity and purity of sound, texture and attack in fast passages as in slow ones, in the more pianistic rhythmic patterns, and in imposing an iron restraint on the innate sensuality and abandon of the violin, Beethoven has in fact achieved a height of violinistic expression more characteristic of the instrument's highest potential than it portrays in any of its more usual incarnations—in the way a great sage is more truly human than ordinary mortals.

1970

For several years, BARTÓK's body had seemed but a thinly taut parchment stretched over a resonant cavity, hollowing itself out with every fatal reverberating pulse; for indeed it existed only to serve the indomitable will of its master—to record and to propagate the vibrations which he captured. This almost intangible body, driven unyieldingly by the varied and fascinating rhythms it had gleaned from the primitive folk-lore of Hungary, the Balkans and the Near East, this determined body was itself but an instrument, in fact symbolically speaking it was a drum, primitive and barbaric, whereon destiny beat its merciless tune. Under the fatal sentence of the disease from which he suffered he lived on borrowed time, each day entrusting more of himself to the spirit, each day surrendering more of his body to the earth, so that when he had traced his final note on the parchment and committed his last echo to the wind, there must have seemed very little left for death to claim.

When great men die—men of the spirit, I mean—our world remains singularly unaffected. One might have searched high and low in New York City on the day that Bartók died for some concrete evidence that a great man, a moving spirit was no more. There was no sign, no tribute; everything seemed quite as usual. Even had one found one's way to the obscure chapel where the last rites were being performed one would have observed a handful of people, curiously dispassionate, lacking in fervour, listening to irrelevant words, uttered in an inappropriate language —for not a word was spoken in his own beloved Hungarian.

That seems to be the way great creative men die—as they fall to earth they cause even less disturbance and produce a smaller ripple than a ripe golden autumn leaf floating down on to the surface of a tranquil lake. And as the leaf, they too have given all their best to the tree, and only the fantastically hued husk remains to melt away. Unlike the fall of a world-leader, which comes as a mighty crash, dragging along with it all those people, things and bodies which were dependent upon and conditioned by the great man, that of our hero was of one who had renounced the world long before he died; his was so gradual a transition from life to death that he seemed to have passed unmourned except by a few faithful disciples. The picture is, however, not quite so dismal from our point of view, for Bartók's works will outlive the Roman baths or the Chinese wall, providing our world survives that long.

The cumulative effect of these mysterious creations of music is incalculable. These great edifices of sound, demanding the utmost in dedication from those who would take time to rebuild them, translating them into living sound according to the indicated plans in the score, are as the mirror to our changing cultures and to our constant passions, wherein we may discover ourselves.

Truly, in the music of Bartók, our age, our world, may discover itself. I use my own case as an illustration. No other contemporary composer has drawn me as irresistibly as Bartók. I felt at one with his implacable and complex rhythms, at one with the abstract yet intensely expressive construction of his melodic lines, at one with his incredibly rich range of harmonies—sometimes simple, sometimes clashing or ironical—and above all at one with that streamlined cleanness of design and execution (always without a trace of irrelevance or sentimentality), just as sharply chiselled and penetrating as his own features and his eyes. One other factor which attracted me irresistibly was the Oriental quality of his music. Bartók steeped himself deeply in the folk-lore of Hungary, the Balkan countries and Asia Minor. He made the most profound study of this music, and organized the scientific classification of many thousands of folk-tunes.

These strong and primitive roots he assimilated into his background, and brought forth with their support a characteristic, genuine and personal style, combining the power of the primitive with the cultivated vision and discourse of the most erudite mind. His knowledge and memory were staggering. His appearance belied the unfathomable fire and power of his character. During his last two years of life (when I knew him), except for the extraordinary precision of his speech and manner, reduced in both cases to a diamond-like sharpness and brilliance with a minimum of motion, gesture or physical effort and a maximum of meaning and intent, his presence gave no evidence of the barbaric grandeur or the mystic vision of his innermost self. Only his eyes, those fantastically piercing eyes, gave him away. They betrayed his fiery soul, while his body, almost consumed, jealously guarded its strength for the most essential tasks.

I shall never forget my first meeting with him; it was in November 1943. Already attracted by the score of his Concerto for Violin before I had even met him or heard any of his music, I had performed this work with Dmitri Mitropoulos and the Minneapolis Symphony Orchestra. Some two weeks later, having programmed his Sonata for Piano and Violin in Carnegie Hall, New York City, I was anxious to play this work for Bartók—to receive his criticism before performing in public. I had arranged to meet him at a friend's home. Immediately I was transported by his burning eyes, and fascinated by the meticulous, immaculate air of this small and wiry creature.

Without further ado, he sat down, produced his spectacles and a pencil, laid out a copy of the Sonata which he had brought along, and, as there were no further formalities, we began. Though I had had no preconceived idea of his manner or appearance, his music had already revealed to me his innermost secrets. A composer is unable to hide anything—by his music you shall know him.

Immediately, with the first notes, there burst forth between us, like an electrical contact, an intimate bond, which was to remain fast and firm. It was as if we had known each other for years. In fact, I believe that between a composer and his interpreter there can exist a stronger, more intimate bond, even without the exchange of words, than between the composer and a friend he may have known all his life. For the composer reserves the core of his personality, the essence of his self for his works.

As we finished the first movement he got up, came over to me and said the following words, which for Bartók were equivalent to an uncontrolled burst of impassioned exuberance: 'I thought works were only played in that way long after the composers were dead.'

I feel particularly privileged to have known this great man during his last years, and happy to have been able to bring him the fervent reverence and devotion of a younger musician. This may, perhaps, in some unconscious way, have assured him that his work and his music would be carried forward through the ages, to inspire and illuminate humanity along its difficult and stony path.

1945

10. Three Modern Masters

GEORGES ENESCO, PABLO CASALS, RAVI SHANKAR

IT WAS IN 1924 that I first saw and heard Georges Enesco when he came to San Francisco from Rumania as a violin soloist and conductor. I was eight years old and I will never forget the impact upon me as he walked on to the stage. I was stunned by his physical presence alone. He was a lion of a man, with a shaggy crown of black hair, tremendously tall and romantic-looking. Then he began to play and I reacted as would an eight-year-old: atavistically, with every part of my being. I had never heard violin-playing like that before. There was, to begin with, the special gipsy quality, an impetuous, emotion-filled expressiveness which is almost a 'parlando' style. He played as if he were improvising the music, with that rapid concentration, that capacity for evoking each note as if it were created afresh out of a nameless void and bore the same significance as words springing to the mind. And, curiously enough, after I had known Enesco for years, once on my mentioning Mozart operas to him, he said 'Perhaps you will now learn to play Mozart as he should be played and understand that every note he composed was like a syllable, a definite gesture, meaning something very specific.' That was indeed how Enesco himself played. All I knew then, at eight years old, was that I must see Enesco again, must hear him play more, must discover the what and why and wherefore of this magical use of the instrument I was just beginning to master.

Three years later in Paris I discovered a poster announcing an Enesco concert and, realizing my longing to know Enesco, my mother and father took me to it, with my two small sisters. At the end of the concert my parents took me backstage. 'Talk to him yourself' they said. I was only eleven and had never accosted anybody entirely on my own. Besides, there was a tremendous crush of fans in his dressing-room. Finally I approached him, terrified, through that chattering jungle. I was utterly unknown, rather small for my age and distinctly plump. 'I would like to study with you,' I said. Always the soul of courtesy, instead of dismissing me offhand as yet another boring small boy with a surely misplaced idea of his own abilities, he said kindly 'I'd love to teach you, I'm sure, but I travel a lot and have very little time. In fact I must leave Paris tomorrow—at six in the morning.' 'All right,' I said, 'I'll come at five.' And so I did, towed by my father, and after I had played for him, he took me as a pupil, refusing any remuneration. From that moment Enesco was a major influence in my life and I was no longer alone. All musicians who knew him, who played with him, will tell you the same: Enesco was one of the greatest inspirations of their lives, musically or otherwise. He drew magical sounds out of orchestras that many another conductor with far more obvious authority never dreamed of, emanating from his enormous breadth of vision and spirit combined with an unusual intensity of musical experience. His was a rare combination of passion and control, each acting upon the other, which refined and humanized an essentially sensual man.

Enesco considered himself 'the laziest man in the world', simply I suppose because he knew neither ambition nor envy, but only the joy of being in the centre of his music, as either violinist, composer, pianist, or conductor—for he was all of that. There were those unforgettable times when he would sit down at an old broken upright piano and, from memory, play the entire score of *Tristan und Isolde*.

As a teacher Enesco perfectly understood the three essential pedagogical problems: where to begin, when to stop, and how to explain what happens in between. It was wonderful for a small boy to study with him for he was full of aesthetic allusions to use as guides. Bach he advised me to play strictly, for he said that however strong your emotional impulse may be, it should never destroy the basic pace nor twist the overall form of the piece from its architectural shape. During one of those lessons in Paris Ravel burst into Enesco's studio. Would Enesco please play his (Ravel's) new piano and violin sonata with him that very evening for the publishers Durand? In those days, unbelievably, music publishers listened to everything first before committing themselves; not even a Ravel was to be trusted unheard (God knows what they do today with dodecaphonic scores). In his usual courteous way, Enesco asked me if I minded waiting, as Ravel's problem was urgent. I sat down fascinated while Ravel (at the piano) and Enesco played through the sonata once. Enesco then asked Ravel to go through it once more 'just to be on the safe side'. Ravel agreed and, to our amazement, Enesco put the score down and, the second time through, played every note from memory.

Soon after the war in 1946 I went to see Enesco in Bucharest. He was no longer young; that immense physique was already beginning to give way. Together we gave ten consecutive days of charity concerts, two each day, rehearsing for hours before each performance. And despite the gruelling work, I do not remember for one moment feeling either stale or tired, so totally inspiring was the effect of working with him again after so many years.

Enesco loved France and England, especially the latter; he could tell you what was characteristically English about a work, teaching me, for example, to understand the tender and innocent quality—that un-Teutonic sentimentality—that fills the music of Elgar. As for France, it was his second country, and even when he was offered every kind of inducement by the People's Republic of Rumania to return there for his last years, he chose to remain at 36 Rue de Clichy in Paris, where he had lived since he was a young man and where he died.

Certainly, as a composer, Enesco never had the wordly success and celebrity he deserved, and I think it was primarily because his chivalrous instincts prevented him from ever aggressively promoting himself or his music. His lovely Rumanian Rhapsodies, composed before he was twenty, are played, but his opera *Oedipus*, Four Symphonies and Octuor for Strings are rarely heard, alas! The Third Sonata for Violin and Piano, nationalist in character, is not only beautiful and unforgettable music, but perhaps the greatest achievement in musical notation I know. What Enesco did miraculously was to transcribe a completely improvisational, spontaneous style on to paper so that it has perfect form and in all respects is an organic entity. Neither simple nor superficial (like a Sarasate 'gipsy' work), anyone who carefully observes every little marking Enesco left in the score will play it exactly the right degree 'out of tune', will perform glissandos at precisely the right spots, and will convey the exact rhythmical attenuations. To be able to score these Rumanian characteristics is like capturing the song of a bird on paper.

Perhaps the essence of Enesco as a man is summed up by the story of his marriage, which reveals all his chivalry and loyalty. When he was in his late teens, he fell in love with one of the great beauties of the Rumanian Court. She was a Princess, older than he and already married. Years later in Paris he announced quite suddenly that he would have to leave because of an urgent matter requiring his attention in Vienna. When he returned he brought the Princess with him—as his wife. By then her own husband had died, her children were married, and she herself was desperately ill. For the rest of his life Enesco cherished La Princesse, as he always called her, with total devotion.

Georges Enesco was above all a man of great loyalty. Perhaps his very essence, his whole quality, was a shade too high for the commercial values of the world as it now is, and his vision far beyond that of most of his colleagues. That is why although his reputation may not be universal, one will never hear an evil word spoken of this great man.

*   *   *   *   *   *

The Lord rewarded me according to my righteousness; according to the cleanness of my hands hath he recompensed me.
Psalm of David to the Chief Musician

Within the pages of *Joys and Sorrows*[1] CASALS appears revealed by his own voice as that ever-rarer human phenomenon, a man who has apparently never experienced an inner struggle, never experienced a divided loyalty, never suffered a torn conscience or known a qualm. Never to have faced 'if', or 'but', or 'perhaps'; never to have wasted a moment on bypaths; to have conserved every bit of energy and movement for the straightforward road. Is it the happy cumulative effect of consonant loyalties—family, patriotic, religious and social—which have conditioned this extraordinary man never to question the first and therefore only right and final answer, or is it a facet of the monolithic Spanish stance?

With a blessed naïveté, as childlike as it is disarming and

[1] by Pablo Casals and Albert E. Kahn (Macdonald 1970).

invulnerable, Casals speaks without conditionals. Not for him are those graduated shades of opinion and behaviour, those shady ambiguities in which the tortured conscience takes refuge.

Uncompromising and dedicated, he was upheld by the devotion, the trust and the love of those whom he in turn loved and trusted. At the very core of his being are those stubborn roots that cling tenaciously to that world which is his and which belongs to him, the very soil of his native Catalonia—the sea and sand, the serrated mountains; the animals—horse, dog, ducks and canaries; the whole range of its people from the manual workers to the poets, composers and monks, from the seamstress to the Queen. And how tightly, how dearly has he clung to all he cherished, tangible and intangible.

What indeed he must have suffered keenly was that searing sense of longing, that nostalgia that overwhelms the exile from a beloved homeland. Yet how wise he was to choose his first refuge in the Basque region of France in a landscape so nearly his own, in the very shadow of his people's Canigou (their sacred mountain). Now again in choosing Puerto Rico he has revealed that infallible sense of one who knows unerringly what he is and where he belongs. How different from the cruel fate of a Bartók, similarly torn by an act of his own volition from his native soil, pacing the hideously noisy and barren streets of New York, longing for a tree, the smell of a horse, for some reassuring and familiar sound!

He is protector and defender by divine compulsion—a latter-day crusader. And how infinitely precious to us all is this shining Don Quixote in his very personal armour and weapons—his bow and baton alike.

Was that first 'cello his father made, little more than a broom-stick strung with strings, not only a musical instrument but also a scourge with which he might sweep the Temple of Music clean of desecration and raise the status of the musician from performer to reformer?

And yet in the very simplicity and directness of his strength there lies a correlative weakness. Admirable, enviable though it be, does it not deny the relative values inherent in truth, ignore the mitigating circumstance that is in all human situations, refuse to condone the infinitely varied admixture of good and evil, selfishness and altruism, that informs and persuades all action? Does he occasionally halt to consider the effect of that most subtle of all devils, Fear, upon strong and weak alike? From the start he himself was embedded in and supported by the royal structure of society, which recognized his own merit and which enabled him almost immediately as a child to be encouraged, educated and befriended by the most influential, generous and cultivated people of his country—and this by his own admission. Does the childlike ingenuousness of those oft-recurring accounts of Queens, Kings, Presidents and Ambassadors waiting deferentially, opening doors for Casals to pass first, standing out in the cold to see him off, confessing their mistakes, betray the classic dichotomy to be found in all Republicans?

Casals' personal life is like one grand sweeping arch, carrying him from the Catalonian sand and sea to the Puerto Rican, from his mother to his mother's homeland—an arch bestriding nearly a century, straight as a die or a Roman road, a life disciplined by the 'cello and its manual exactions, restored, renewed daily and inspired by Bach's music and the great classics, animated by an indefatigable zest for and love of all life, supported by an infinite and delightful capacity for enjoying the beauties of nature, lightened by a quiet sense of humour, a life *engaged* from its first hours, working, talking, playing, engaged in every conceivable way and impelled by a burning zeal to further, to give and to inspire.

But what constitutes the greatness in a performing musician is not only his ability to connect his music to the universal, the fundamental in all life, but also his attention to the pure mechanics of playing in terms of both technique and instinct. That Casals has both faculties is evident from the first moment of working with him, and if I may be forgiven for mentioning my own personal experiences with him, it was total joy during those many seasons in Prades, and again latterly in Puerto Rico, to be part of his wonderful ambience, to find oneself guided, supported, uplifted in the trios and quartets we played with that ineffable sense of the rightness of all he suggested, the musical purity and certainty of his approach.

Casals must remain a constant, unflickering light, strong, and unyielding, impervious to the merely expedient, as to the vulgar

or makeshift; uncontaminated, undefiled by any sort of compromise with brute power, with tyranny, or with commercialism.
His supreme and loyal dedication to his 'manual work', as he likes
to call it, his art, his people, his land, his trenchant and clear-cut
thoughts, convictions and actions, his personal and social disciplines all mark him out as the rarest of men, as pure of heart
at 93 as he was when a child; frugal, abstemious within reason;
simple, stubborn, loyal, lovable, shrewd, unerring in the particular
sense of his life's direction: in fact, the highest incarnation of the
wise man of the earth, wise in truth and at one with himself and
God.

* * * * * *

To the Indian quality of serenity, the Indian musician brings an
exalted personal expression of union with the infinite, as in
infinite love. Few modern composers in the West have achieved
this quality, though we revere it in the works of Bach, Mozart,
and Beethoven. Perhaps we should not admonish our contemporary composers for having lost this sense of serene
exaltation, for indeed we have little enough of it in our civilization
for them to draw upon; yet what quality is music, the organization
of pure sounds, better suited to express? If the Indian musicians
who are now beginning to bring their genius to us—musicians
like RAVI SHANKAR—can help us to find this quality again,
then we shall have much to thank them for.

The appeal that Ravi Shankar exercises over our youth—the
magic aura his presence and his music evoke—is a tribute both
to his great art and to the intuitive wisdom of the searching young.

In him they recognize a synthesis of the immediacy of expression, the spontaneity, truth and integrity of action suited to
the moment, which is a form of honesty characteristic of both the
innocent child and the great artist. In him they see the mastery
and dedication of a discipline born of infinite experience and
concentrated effort that are manifestations not only of the artist's
own being but of the generations preceding him.

Human history can be seen as though revealed to us by mirrors,
mirrors at first small and dim, by which man could barely discern
his aspect or his motives, mirrors that grew ever larger, revealing
man to himself and as he appeared to others. With each increase

in size and accuracy, the image seemed more awesome and frightening, until finally today mirrors are looming larger than man himself, and seem actually to dwarf him. That other inner mirror, our conscience, which expressed itself in religion and law, has become in many parts of the world monstrously enlarged to include informers and hangmen—betrayers—who almost outnumber their working, wretched victims. In *our* society, the outer mirror, the mirror reflecting ourselves to others or others to ourselves, has in the public-relations image also become monstrously enlarged, to the point that advisers and experts—manipulators—almost outnumber their clients.

This compulsive need to consult our mirrors—to find inner and outer approval (or, if not approval, at least justification), to be able to face at all times either a jury or a pack of journalists with ready statement—has now reached absurd proportions.

The artist who knows it all too well himself is now an 'ambassador', a 'high priest', an 'innovator', a 'cultural artifact'— he behaves like one, looks like one. In a debased sense he is shown as the end and the means, the alpha and omega, and is in danger of becoming a crystallized symbol covering an empty gesture, like Aubry's ghost disappearing on approach with a 'most melodious twang'. Yet, thanks be to God, at the moment of genuine creation there is an incandescence that dissolves all impurities, leaving only burnished gold.

When mastery will reward them, the mirrors will fall away and the elect will know that sensation of rightness which is independent of witness. They will achieve the creative purity and innocence in which 'I am as I am' is 'I do as I do'.

Ravi Shankar has brought me a precious gift. Through him I have added a new dimension to my experience of music—one which belongs to all great music, including our own, but which, along with so much that should remain inspired and intuitive, is blueprinted out of our world.

But to the young people, who give their mind and heart to Ravi Shankar's art, he has made sense and brought order out of chaos, for he has restored the fundamental and supreme value of dedicated work, of self-control, of faith and of the value of living.

1970

11. The Music of India

I FEEL THAT the growing fascination which the music and dance of India exert upon us indicates more than the physical consequence of our much-vaunted communications era. It is rather the mysterious urge to return to sources, together with a search for yardsticks beyond the confines of familiar values. These arts, representing aesthetic and philosophical views, these disciplines and techniques evolved on sound physiological and emotional principles, are thousands of years old. They are in fact the oldest living forms of man's title to divinity, creating order and beauty for the ear and the eye of the purest and most dedicated quality.

England has known for well-nigh a thousand years a high level of order and influence, and its unbroken continuity has absorbed the impact of upheavals. But other national histories are marked by spasmodic fits and starts, by self-generating revolutionary deaths and rebirths, and by the effort of wiping clean every time every vestigial reminder—in person, place or thing—of a former order. Each time the past is obliterated and a new cycle started, which in its turn is condemned to the same end. Periodically, then, each new embodiment represents almost as much of a loss as a gain.

The last of these upheavals, in which we still find ourselves, is the result of the release through knowledge of ever greater sources of energy. The application and harnessing of various forms of power have at each stage afforded the country concerned a physical and economical ascendancy over others. Although this power has sent our various flags over the seven seas, it has tended, as unchallenged power often does, to isolate us from the cultures of the newly explored lands, and also from the long familiar cultures of the countries from which we set sail. In spite of hundreds of years of association between their countries, Dutch

'Knight of the British Empire' 1965

Above: Cambridge 1970, Honorary Doctor of Music.

Early
Portrait

women have not achieved the grace in movement of the Balinese, nor is there the slightest trace of Indian modes in the stirring music of Elgar.

Culturally speaking we gave much and took little. Not only did England give the great language which now enables India to hold such an articulate place in the family of nations, but equally it gave those principles of government by consent which have enabled India to formulate a Constitution second to none. It is a pity that in exchange she missed the opportunity to explore and exploit the vast artistic traditions inherent in the music and dancing of this ancient continent, but preferred to remain aloof.

During this last phase of our development, however, a subtle but profound change has been wrought. Knowledge which in restricted periods and regions has time and again been won and lost, has finally achieved a degree of concentration sufficiently strong and widespread to survive on its own, and to break its parochial confines, in spite of the struggles, diseases and disasters which mankind is for ever bringing upon itself. It is now able to accumulate—to grow—in unbroken continuity, almost in defiance of mankind.

We have pursued our search for power, in a line from Prometheus to its ultimate conclusion, proving thereby in harsh reality the particle theory of matter, as well as the equation of matter and energy, which, incidentally, was divined philosophically thousands of years ago in India. We have found that knowledge has, in a sense, defeated our more selfish ambitions—while it has led us along the garden path—by its very qualities of universality and objectivity. It is in fact reducing our lead over the Oriental and African races rather than extending it. Having along our own path, in our own way, reached that point—so often reached by ancient philosophies—where our knowledge, theoretical or practical, demands equation with living man, we should be in the frame of mind to search for those principles of life which by implication our new knowledge demands.

Knowledge may have achieved an independent serenity, a life of its own, but as living human beings we still yearn for continuity and beauty and for a glimpse of the infinite. We search this spinning sphere, and where should we come to rest more naturally than in those places where a single cultural strand based on cumulative experience—meditative as well as practical—has existed unbroken for over three thousand years? What more natural than that the two arts (the impalpable and the palpable, the intangible vibration of sound and the tangible movements of the body) of the music and dance of India should so powerfully and mysteriously attract us?

Humanity is very gradually beginning to conceive a world in terms of the relation between all things and phenomena, instead of in terms of isolated things and phenomena, and to distinguish basic directions of motion. One of the most popular studies today is anthropology, together with other comparative social and technical sciences in the realms of music and medicine. Our knowledge is gradually approaching the stage at which art and science are indissolubly wedded. Not until this process is complete can humanity as a whole achieve harmony. To an extraordinary extent this marriage is to be found in Indian classical music, in which the musician improvises freely, although in accordance with and within a very strict order of melody and metre.

From time immemorial, and indeed until two generations ago, races have wandered freely and bloods have mixed. The Orient had long influenced our thought in science, theology, astronomy. The Moslems served as a connecting link all the way from Indonesia to Spain. The Mongols penetrated to Hungary, the Caucasian tribes very probably to Peru, the Moors to the shores of the Atlantic; and the Negroes, somewhat less willingly but all the more effectively carried their rhythm, their natural abandon and spirit from Africa to the far coasts of both Americas.

The rising barriers of severely defined national boundaries in Western Europe, together with the growth of industry, which increased national power, interrupted this process, and the damming of this free intercourse reached its apogee in the Nazi and Fascist theories of race purity. Today, at least on the artistic and intellectual level, we are witnessing a renewal of the cross-breeding of cultures, both in order to counteract the reactionary attitude of the nineteenth century, and also from a thirst for fresh inspiration and a need for new creative impetus. We can trace this tendency as far back as Debussy, and more recently in Bartók and Benjamin Britten.

This trend holds great promise for humanity, for we have much to learn in many fields from both the theoretical and the empirical knowledge which in India and China, and other ancient cultures, comes to us from a still unbroken past. In Indian religion the body and soul have never been separated; and when they come to music, which is still mainly a votive offering, Indians believe in its therapeutic quality as well as in its spiritual effect. By the same token they have not submitted to our even-tempered scale. Our own chromatic scale, which had its beginning with Bach, has served us well in portraying ever more intensely and dramatically the passion and emotion of the individual and the group, until we have reached in the last generation a revulsion against the over-graphic, which has in its turn prepared the way for a music at once more abstract and less personal.

Here I feel is where the eclectic and highly evolved character of Indian music has finally become significant to the Western ear. Indian music has always stressed the relation of man to the universal. For this purpose the modal composition—cast in one mood, on a fixed base, of which the intervals are carefully matched and selected, together with a particular rhythmic pattern—is capable of achieving a progressive and irresistible hypnotic effect, in the sense that it liberates the higher mind from the limits of physical form. So long as we have not studied and tabulated the specific effects of particular scales (modes) and particular intervals, our efforts at musical therapy can only remain rudimentary and haphazard. This distinction in degree and kind between the personal and the universal is most urgent in our day, when these dimensions seem hopelessly entangled. While our common and fundamental aims remain divided and fragmented we suffer from the standardization of culture instead of enjoying its diversification.

It seems to me that the trend lies along the basic direction I have outlined, although only a small minority is aware of it. Certainly, as might be expected, interest in Indian music is at its highest in England, although it is not lagging far behind in the United States, where the element of curiosity has always been part of one's intellectual equipment. Conversely, however, it is most discouraging to note the lack of interest, respect and understanding in the attitude of the Eastern peoples themselves towards their own unique cultural heritage, and their haste to jettison it in their eagerness to imitate our scales and harmonies. It would appear that national ambitions and technological progress go hand in hand with the tonic-dominant harmonies of the Sousa march! It is rather as though they felt that the dancing figures on the wonderful façades of the temples of Orissa and Ellora would be improved by the addition of boots and shoes. In my capacity of President of the Asian Music Circle I am continually faced with this shortsighted attitude, and have often felt that it may fall upon us in the West, our anthropologists, musicians and composers, painters and poets to rescue such knowledge, art and wisdom as these Eastern and now African countries have failed to destroy themselves.

What is the fundamental dilemma now facing the musicians of India and their 3,000-year-old art? This is the question I would now like to consider.

The Indian musician is essentially an independent artisan, living in what must still be the least compulsive society in the world. Their individual disciplines arose as the expression of a natural order, the interplay between the will of God and the will of man, and not as the result of the will of men upon men.

Of all great countries, India has certainly the most creative population, enjoying a diversity and variety wellnigh indescribable and possessing a minimum of standardized procedures or stereotyped beliefs. This is as true of their music as of all else. Each violin-player plays his instrument with a somewhat different hold and fingering. Their remarkable flute-player Ghosh, who died recently, had evolved a large bamboo flute with the most haunting of deep sounds. No two flutes are anywhere exactly alike.

Whatever material or physical difficulties the Indian may have to endure, at least the specific psychological and physical diseases of our too conventionalized existence, attendant upon endless duplication and superfluity, are as yet largely absent from this civilization.

Here are millions of free-wheeling individuals held together, to be sure, by the oldest unbroken culture and spiritual patterns, but none the less attached symbolically, not to wheels enmeshed as it were in a common gear-box and driving a particular machine in some given direction, but attached rather to individual separate prayer-wheels, each a motion unto itself.

So long as the musician and his art remained at the temples in the service of God (or of one of their many lesser deities), a practice that obtained until relatively recently, much as in our own musical culture until the time of Bach, or again, as they and we did more recently still, in the service of a small and cultivated aristocracy or a particular prince, this introspective and highly sophisticated music could still unfailingly cast its meditative spell and establish the necessary communion between men and a higher power.

Except for a few 'set' compositions by a few outstanding composers, all Indian music is still improvised. Again, as with our own ancient music, the composer and the performer were one, with the essential difference that our musicians often committed their works to paper. This process is really not essential in a world in which each individual is on an almost solitary lifelong search for an aesthetic and spiritual state of balanced perfection. With us, the implacable growth of the social unit, as reflected in the movement from unison to counterpoint, to harmony, to chromaticism and finally to the breakdown of all tonal reference points, made it necessary, indeed essential to copy our parts. In fact, in quite a few works by Mozart and his predecessors only the parts and not the score were written by the composer, so little did he need the score and so much did the performers need the parts.

Now, as I write, our own modern world has caught up with the Indian, with its organized demands and split-second mass timings, its stress on mass culture and mass entertainment, and its preoccupation with colours in all spheres.

Whereas our musical forms grew in size and volume over a period of 500 years, more or less in proportion with the growth of the enlightened public audience and the average-sized concert halls and opera houses, the Indian musician has been catapulted from his private reverie at the foot of a temple, his dedicated obeisance to his gods, on to a wooden scaffolding draped in bunting, hung with microphones and entertaining an audience of 15,000—as at the Thiagaraja Festival in Madras, where musicians came from near and far to meet each other, often sacrificing their fees. This mass celebration, held during the prolonged dry seasons with their glorious nights, is possible only thanks to electronic amplification and its dubious benefits.

Although at these manifestations you could hear a pin drop, as the saying goes, the question still remains whether in the long run the unique and exalted phenomenon squatting on the rostrum, oblivious of external time and place, will adequately express the multiple tensions, aspirations, and passions of the new society.

The composer-performer, both intellectual and manual craftsman, is not as free to experiment in the abstract as the specialist composer, who is unfettered by the confining techniques of a particular instrument, and especially of such specifically melodic instruments as the Indian ones. Even our well-tempered piano, which has been the beast of burden of all (good- and bad-tempered) Western composers, is completely unsuitable for Indian music and utterly alien to the Indian temperament.

In fact, when one's ears become attuned to Indian music the very sound of a keyed instrument seems intolerably crude. It is, incidentally, less so with the combination of harpsichord and violin which, together with Monteverdi or Josquin des Prés, and the works of Bartók, form the very best bridge to the traditional Indian audience.

Recently, overlooking the more recent and sophisticated trends in the West and confusing 'westernization' with 'modernization', a particularly untimely and embarrassing effort has been made to band twenty or thirty Indian instruments together, creating 'orchestras' and requiring 'conductors'. This is altogether ludicrous, and does violence to the very nature of Indian classical music. This is owing to some curious time-lag between West and East, just at the moment when we in the West have begun to shun the super-colossal, the extravagant duplication, whose sole reason for existence is one of size and quantity rather than of finesse and quality.

The optimum number of Indian instruments that may be harnessed together is probably five or six, which Lukas Foss has found out to be approximately the maximum number of players capable of improvising together, each carrying a unique one-voice-to-a-line responsibility.

The duplication (not to speak of multiplication by three or

more) of instruments merely adds dead weight and hampers the infinitely delicate, sinuous and ornamental qualities of the Indian musical idiom.

When a violinist plays the Paganini Concerto, or even the Brahms or Tchaikovsky, a certain flourish of his ego is desirable, not to say indispensable (though obviously not in the case of Bach or Beethoven). In Indian music this element is almost completely foreign, so that it is a serious matter for the Indian artist to decide how far he should go in playing to the gallery. It is not that he is incapable of communicating mood or emotion. Quite the contrary. But this communication between artist and audience sharing a common spiritual background will be terribly cheapened with the dissolution of their heritage and will lead to extravagant and flashy attempts by the artist to retain his audience's concentration.

Apart from this enthusiastic revival, and the nation's new pride in their own Indian musical heritage following the independence of the country, neither the period of British rule nor the present economic, commercial and nationalistic ambience have been conducive to the optimum survival of Indian music in its present crystallized form.

Although a few Indian musicians have achieved great popularity in their own country as well as internationally, as for instance Ravi Shankar, Ali Akbar Khan and Alla Rakha, and also such dancers as Shanta Rao and Idrani (the latter is half-American), the great bulk of admirable but lesser-known artists, on whom after all the whole structure of Indian art depends, live in great difficulty. An outstanding instrument-maker can barely make ends meet as most musicians are too poor to afford his instruments.

While it is true that All-India Radio, under the enlightened guidance of Narayana Menon, the Deputy Director, maintains several musicians permanently and several hundred others intermittently, what is this number after all in a nation of 438 million? The enormous Indian film industry (the second largest in the world) also engages numerous musicians, but here again they are obliged as a rule to compromise the traditions and the standards which are their heritage.

Traditionally shunning organized societies, not to speak of labour unions, the Indian musician today is caught between two

stools, i.e. between a tradition now becoming uncontemporary
and an economic and social status below his cultivated and rare
talents. Fortunately the sheer breadth of this vast subcontinent,
together with the life-habits of its aesthetic and stylistically conscious people, offer a time-margin to Indian music during which
a renewed interest and appreciation of their great musical art
may be fostered.

Meanwhile Indian music and Indian musicians are of immense
benefit to us in the West: to our listeners, to our composers, and
to our scholars, contributing as they do to a better understanding of our own ancient music, particularly in its ornamentation, and its melody and rhythmic aspects. Certainly in my
experience there are no musicians anywhere with a keener or more
critical approach to a more refined or sophisticated art. I would
say without hesitation that the Indian musician possesses easily
the most acute and accurate sense of hearing and pitch, as well
as the most evolved sense of rhythm, of any the world over.
Perhaps we may return these benefits by a second cross-fertilization,
which while not damaging the roots and trunk of the tree of
Indian music, will yet bring forth wonderful fruit.

In fact, just as India has stepped into the atomic age directly
from the bullock age, its nuclear physicists finding absolutely no
contradiction between the timeless philosophy of their people and
the tenets and implied philosophy of Einstein's matter-energy
world, so I believe will their musicians successfully bypass the
cruder manifestations of the nineteenth century's industrialization
and bombast, comfortably joining their tone-rows with ours, and
bringing their own invaluable contributions in terms of rhythmic
and melodic complexities as yet undreamt of by us. Their free
improvisation will no doubt be applied not only to 'conventional'
music but to electronic music as well, for which I would wager
they are supremely gifted, aware as they are of the numerical and
numerological, and of the infinite subdivision and transformation
of all elements.

1962

Part Two: Education

12. The Compleat Education

I HAVE USED this quaint term rather than the modern one as the modern spelling and modern usage, together with most things contemporary, does not allow for mysteries unsolved and unfulfilled: in the naked brutal light of our 'factual' disciplines, 'complete' might be taken at its literal value, whereas in fact there is no such thing as a 'complete' education. To be complete, education in its widest sense would have to include all experience.

My inspiration derives from a sixteenth-century volume entitled *The Compleat Housewife,* which contains recipes for cooking and brewing, medicine and hygiene—but even so, knowing, as I do from all that my wife achieves, the myriad and complex microcosm that is a housewife's world, I can assure you all that not a dozen books would do justice to the compleat housewife.

Traditional education concentrates almost exclusively on man's relatively recently acquired mental techniques, abandoning the so-called 'irrational', ancient and fundamental thought-forms to the mercies of natural environment, social pressures, or hereditary influence, which as often as not remain unexpressed.

Of all activities which come closest to harnessing the whole man, violin-playing would seem to me as good an example as any, enlisting as it does all man's faculties.

These faculties derive, I suggest, from four fields of experience:

1. Man versus infinity—versus that chain of life and death, stretching into eternity and infinity on both sides of his life and all around; or in other words, man versus all that he can never understand. Religion and philosophy, as well as those moments of ecstasy or vision, of self-sacrifice and inner peace—the saint, the mystic, and to a degree every mother and every teacher, reflect this orientation. This is man spiritual, and all that part of his physical self which obeys

79

powers higher than those of his own personal will to survival.

2. Man versus his physical environment—light, air, water, earth, food, rhythm, height, sound, smell, as reported by his senses; these lead to survival and the sensations of pleasure and pain. By these impressions every gesture, act, word, sound, taste, etc., acquires a personal flavour or colour either tempting or repellent. This is man physical, together with all his mental and emotional existence concerned with personal survival or pleasure. These are of course not by any means always synonymous—which fact leads to much inner travail. Nor are my four categories conceivable in isolation—they remain inter-dependent, co-existent and continually demanding adjustment and reconciliation.

3. Man versus other men or other life—family, tribe, community, race or nation, or all living co-inhabitants of the earth. This is man social.

4. Man versus himself—not in the sense of survival, but as an instrument of which he is the chief artist and player, an instrument which he must perfect in every conceivable way —obedient and expressive of his will, instinct, intelligence and emotion—resembling perhaps some beautifully trained and wonderful domestic animal. This involves conscience, physical and mental disciplines, order, meditation, perfection of craft. This is man as self.

Contradiction, confusion and conflict result from the interplay of these four categories, and man's whole history has been an effort to reconcile and integrate them.

Only life at its fullest and art at its greatest draw equally on all these fields. During our lifetime it would appear that only at the very beginning do we have anything like a complete education. For in the womb our four fields of experience are admirably condensed:

1. Infinity is reduced to manageable proportions.
2. Natural environment is controlled (beyond the dream of the most advanced totalitarian regime).
3. Other people are no problem (unless there happens to be a twin nuisance, social life is fairly simple).
4. Self-discipline is unnecessary (temptation still unborn).

But until a little while ago, man lived his allotted life-span within a man-made womb which allowed him a sense of finite security, and which crystallized, as it were, in symbolism his too-fluid doubt and fancy:

1. The church and its ecclesiastical hierarchy represented his relation to the infinite.
2. He had overcome his natural environment just sufficiently to feel reasonably secure, so long as he worked hard.
3. He *belonged* to a specific niche in some large feudal family, attached to some established, assigned function from earliest years.
4. And finally, the Pandora's box of his own self had not as yet been further revealed by Freud and others—nor was relativity born. He still knew exactly when he was right or wrong, good or evil. By excluding infinity, and relativity, and by thinking in terms of flat square areas, he was able to place and judge himself with simple tools and measures. He enjoyed the illusion of truth and security, and could take pride in his abstract constructions, however unreal they might be.

Today man is born anew, out of his own second man-made womb—he has sprung the sides, a kind of self-perpetrated caesarian performed from within!—and finds himself in as strange, as bewildering a world as when he first left the security of his mother's womb. Education is a process dramatically opposite to the 'conditioning' properties of the womb. But man for ever wishes to return to the security and fastness of the womb, however blind it be. So, as I see it today, the race is between education and conditioning. Conditioning attempts to transform a living human being into a predictable automaton, conditioned to react in a particular way to a given set of situations.

But as living matter is unpredictable, particularly in the case of human beings, who are to a definite extent self-propelled and self-determining—and as this inherent motion cannot ever be included in any 'conditioning' equation—all efforts at *control*, whether by prevention (conditioning people to predictable reactions, producing herds) or by correction (by means of, for instance, fear and terror, producing mobs) are eventually doomed to failure.

Education aims at the opposite. Education should enable us to meet any free circumstance with a sporting chance of success. But to do this education must include all four fields of experience.

The Inca Indian of Peru, conditioned to the highlands of the Andes, perishes miserably at sea level; and the scholar or scientist must usually be protected in a controlled environment from both —for the mind cannot actually breathe, eat or walk, but can only direct these activities.

Education, unlike conditioning, need not provide prefabricated experience for every occasion or purpose, but should develop an alert, flexible mind and body, not easily taken by surprise. No doubt transition from womb to freedom should be gradual, and even at the age of ten to fifteen it is good for a child to find itself in a complete world, though not yet an open world. This is where the English public school at its best is so remarkable. It is a complete microcosm of human society, already made, yet continually and paradoxically in the making, and a boy graduating from such a school should be able to establish a complete human community in any part of the world, whereas a day-school boy, attending for subjects only, may take the structure and formation of society for granted. Too often—in the absence of compensating influences in the home—our education brings forth predators and parasites. Certain forces in modern society are opposed to such traditional and tried formative agents, without knowing how to separate and choose permanent hard-won values from the transient fashion or symbol.

Totalitarian régimes are altogether opposed to the four fields of human experiences referred to above—namely:

1. Religion—they have an 'ersatz'.
2. Free natural environment—they *control* it.
3. Family—they form groups as *they* choose.
4. Introspection or self-analysis—a heresy to be ruthlessly condemned.

Today the danger of totalitarian conditioning is great, owing to the breakdown of these four categories of experience, and their synthetic substitutes. Human passion, ecstasy, human imagination, vision, the human irrational would appear to find nowhere legitimate avenues of expression. Nor does the human impulse to sacrifice itself for something greater than itself find a proper daily mode of sublimation.

Totalitarian conditioning it would seem in this one respect is ahead of democratic education in that it does take the whole human being into account. Providing a false rationale, it crystallizes the irrational base of all reaction into one dominant love and one dominant hate, as all sweetness in one sugar and all sharpness in one salt, instead of a thousand savours in all strengths. And now other societies, tainted by this over-simplification instead of respecting life and living beings for themselves, in their infinite variety, reduce these to one ideal or a succession of ideals, and instead of a thousand comfortable, relatively harmless little prejudices we must now hate nothing less than all the capitalists, all the communists, all the Jews or blacks or Christians, and so forth.

I remember, as a child, visiting the Chelsea Flower Show, where I found a plethora of smells; today there are hardly any. This is as ominous a pointer as any towards our contemporary trend of synthesizing all phenomena to a single salient feature, as 'Flowers for Show'.

We seem to be losing our sense of variety as well as the overall linking of one unit to another, the past to the future, the interaction between smell and taste: this in favour of a dissection of isolated instances and isolated individuals. In a kind of destructive madness we would lay bare, as under the microscope, every inch of gut and viscera we can expose, both literally and figuratively. But continuity is more than a succession of instants, and life is more than a string of facts.

Unless the instant can be related to the whole, until the smallest detail can take its rightful place in the total scheme of things, until I—the individual—know where I belong and what function I fulfil, I will remain a disassociated specimen instead of a living part of the whole.

This is all the more difficult as the very material we are dealing with is not inert, is not mud or clay; it is self-propelled, and each little unit, though fitting into the motion of another unit, none the less has its own motion; and this motion unto itself is the factor that is too often overlooked, and which must be taken into the general calculation.

We are therefore concerned with totality even as we are concerned with its smallest fraction. Education is the total of all the impressions we receive. But as we cannot provide a total form in any definite or defined series of studies or accumulation of impressions, we must sketch in this total, and those little corners that we fill in with our one-sided education must always be seen in their relationship to all that remains unfulfilled in our very vague sketch.

Conditioning, as I said earlier, is in a sense the opposite of education. Conditioning would seek to fill in in black and white those corners I spoke of, in an arbitrary way, and simply exclude —as if that were possible—everything that is not absolutely controllable and definable. Conditioning eventually always defeats itself, because the unknown, the mysterious will have its say; will rear its head at some time or other, simply because it exists. The great 'it' which must for ever remain unexplainable must always be considered a silent partner of all our doings, of all that we think, and of every act in our lives.

Conditioning attempts to make motion predictable, but as we have seen, motion is not completely predictable because it is a combination of that motion which is calculable and that element which is either random or self-willed: conditioning must always fail. Man more than any living thing has this capacity for self-determination—in other words, he can determine his own motion to a degree. As this is the accumulated heritage of a long, long struggle to become independent, to control his own life, it is not likely to be surrendered easily, although it has to be defended with every breath he takes.

Let us consider the largest canvas, and therefore the greatest space, which, in the absence of guide-lines, becomes the most dangerous vacuum—that of man versus infinity. With the abdication of formal traditional symbols and rituals, we tend to forget what these stood for. The mistake comes about when men usurp symbols. This is a contradiction in terms, for the symbol standing for the infinite should not become the private property of man. But every symbol created by man gradually becomes the possession of a particular private group, and eventually men are

found fighting over something of which they basically know nothing. We each have a particular and private form of ignorance which seems dearer to us than life itself. But what about the conception which is still there, and still demands recognition of a kind? Respect for old symbols should go hand in hand with the new ones we continually create, or should create. The great masterpieces of architecture, of music and painting—why can they not continue to serve as such symbols even as we add to them, as each generation produces new ones? Are these not the durable materials with which man may span the succeeding generations? For what are mysteries of art and philosophy other than problems of which the basic measurable unit or dimension is larger than a single life, or even many lives and deaths? Beyond our senses, or at least our survival senses, beyond our lifetime, beyond our reasoning, there is always present the mysterious, infinite eternity. It is against this infinite that surrounds every living moment that we measure our progress, our gain or loss; for it surrounds us as the great ocean envelops the slithering fish. True, we learn more and more about this ocean, and even about oceans beyond oceans; but make no mistake—as our knowledge expands so does the realm of mystery.

For this infinity and eternal mystery we need symbols: and what more wonderful expressions of the symbolic can be imagined than cathedrals, temples or mosques, the large and small houses of worship that have been created for this very purpose? Whatever future embodiments of the concept of infinity may await mankind, they must all have in common a capacity to give to every man, woman and child that sense of the mystery of which we are an essential part. This can only happen in a 'holy' place—a place where the greater dimension holds sway to the exclusion of all concerns with immediate survival, with getting the better of our fellow-men, with our petty ambitions and fears. Such a place must be noble in its proportions, serene and inspiring. For communal purposes and for society it must be a man-made edifice; for the individual, however, a hilltop or almost any place should serve. For these symbols to be socially valid they must not only embody an inheritance from the past, but they must also be a product of a living power—urgent and vital. Simply to destroy past symbols is brutal and ignorant. Men destroy and fight because they have a compulsion to do something together, and this at least is an activity which is free (you only pay later). Because man has a rational mind, he will always find good reasons for fighting; how often is the rational mind enslaved by the irrational urge! Of course, the overriding justification is fear of the other fellow. It is not fighting *per se* I mistrust, for the will to fight is healthy fuel; but the engine must be directed by a *right* mind, not simply a rational one.

As like breeds like, war breeds war, pain generates pain, love love, hate hate and so on, it is up to our education to train and teach us how to break the inevitable cycles and start better ones; otherwise it merely makes us cleverer at our own destruction. We have seen the ways in which some of us have lost our sense of relation with infinity, but we have also lost it in the second field I mentioned—that of our physical environment. As often as not, behaviour, custom, ambition are dictated by an altogether arbitrary and exclusive criterion such as money, or a particular fashion of acquisition or apparel. This is no different from that of certain African tribes, the *ne plus ultra* of whose women's ambition is to develop buxom buttocks. It is the stressing of one particular criterion—and an arbitrary one at that—which seems to give man his sense of superiority over mere animals. But the very quality of man is that he is not physically specialized in any form of survival, but is in fact the most vulnerable of all animals. His very nature demands that he must take into account a complex and fluid environment to which there is no single response. At the same time we have lost direct contact with our physical environment, which would at least give us the accurate measure of ourselves as animals—and perhaps not only in the lowest sense, but aesthetically too. I say this because I would maintain that the human body at its highest development of usefulness and elegance is the basic measure of aesthetic proportion and of the sense of the beautiful. I am sure that the Greeks would never have achieved nobility of architecture had they not first had the particular ideal of physical beauty in man and woman.

Let us look at the third field, that is, man in relation to his fellow-men. At one time the family, or the enlarged family of the tribe, or the feudal community, contained complete relationships; within this unit everyone knew his place and function. Gradually these ties, these biological, physiological, hereditary ties have been dissolved, though the first shall certainly be the last—that is, the family. Though we may evolve to become spacemen with minds only, I doubt if so long as there is such a creature as a human being he will be divorced from the reality of his physical environment, or from his family, or his community feeling. At the present moment, social relationships have become so detached that in this respect another vacuum has been created. This vacuum other systems attempt to fill by an arbitrary association of people for specific jobs, in the way that workers in a certain trade join together to form a union. Such an association is valid only in the proportion to which that particular job is a proportion of our lives. In other words our total intellectual, emotional, physical life is certainly far greater than the particular job of, say, the worker in a toothpaste factory. Therefore our terms of reference as regards both the physical environment and the community environment need to be far wider than merely the association with our fellow toothpaste-factory workers.

General ideas, instead of remaining complex and fluid, open to influence and searching for wide horizons, often become solidified in such associations. As ideas become solidified, so does a collective madness spread, for people shrink from the real complexities which they cannot comprehend; eventually they commit themselves to one idol, one superstition or one creed. Real education must be the very contrary of this process. It must teach us to weigh and to compare, to analyse ourselves, to inoculate ourselves with every possible germ. We are capable of building antibodies against disease, and above all can cultivate a sense of values—physical (which we have already spoken about), moral, aesthetic and social.

We have now referred to the first three fields I mentioned, and finally we have the last one to consider—man versus himself. Today the obligation to work is less compulsive than it has ever been before. This is why I put such a high value on craft, on the playing of the violin, if you wish—on any kind of art which engages the whole of an individual. As one learns to manipulate the material (and the more sensitive and elusive that material, the greater the refinement will be for the individual who tries to work with it) one achieves a sense of the possible and of the impossible.

One also learns how long it takes to cultivate perfection, and how empty and vain it is to storm at difficulties, to assail the establishment with passion and fury, to try to tear down—as if the building were something to be taken for granted. Tearing down is important from time to time, but before we tear down we must know what we wish to build instead. It should be something more noble, worthy of the best in man, and if it is not then it is better to remodel slowly in order to improve what we have, and not destroy what it has taken human beings much suffering and much patience to erect.

We must learn to work and to fight for a real object. By a real object, I mean one of our own choice, and which aims to improve ourselves as much as to alter our environment. It must be something practical, close to ourselves, close to each individual—something which demands that we make a good tool of ourselves for the purpose. If we fail in this, we shall find ourselves dumb tools in someone else's hands. We must learn to recognize the difference between an ideal that is useful and one that is not. The irrational and the ideal are related: they are an integral part of every smallest bit of matter which aspires to light and consummation. A useful ideal makes us wish, for example, to improve a difficult social situation, to make an ugly street more pleasant, to make ourselves into better tools, more beautiful and refined. Such an ideal helps us to keep illness at bay, to achieve a balanced existence for humanity. These are the ideals to be carried away from a university.

To students at a university, I would say this. You must emerge from your adolescence with a colossal urge to make yourselves and your world a better place. You must also have the capacity to deny yourself something for a greater good. Don't count on gratitude or recognition, don't try for credit, don't say 'were I in his place'—you are not; proceed rather to understand the situation from the assumption that in his place you might do neither better nor worse, and might even conceivably do exactly as he does. Don't assume superiority. Remember that life is not ready-made, consisting only of ready-made houses, cars, bottles or books. It is what you make of it; and unless you yourself do make something of it, someone else or something else will, and then you will be just a slave in his hands. Don't think in terms of that common denominator money, which is extremely useful but has no intrinsic value. I don't by any means wish to disparage the function that money fulfils—in fact I would ascribe more of democratic development, of equality between human beings, to money than to any other single agent. It is a fact that a coin purse has the same value regardless of which pocket it is in. It may have made one pocket as good as another, but its true function still depends upon the purpose to which it is applied, and upon those values which have no commercial market.

In this connection, I would like to clear up one basic misconception, which is now particularly true of the general mentality of the twentieth century, and was at one time more true of Western than of Eastern philosophy. This is the philosophy that one thing can only live at the expense of another. Our capitalist system, thanks to the large-scale production which became possible with the Industrial Revolution, has already shown that it is in fact the speed and scale of turnover that maintains economic standards. It is not one motor-car at the expense of another, it is rather that one motor-car breeds another. The same is true in India, where traditionally monkeys, birds and cows are allowed to propagate and proliferate without being slaughtered. Actually the animals contribute to the fertility of the soil. The cycle has been expanded to include more life of various kinds so that it can sustain more life, the cycle being greater and the speed of turnover corresponding. The philosophy of 'one thing at the expense of another' holds true only where you have an enclosed, restricted space. For example, the oxygen in a submarine will last only a definite time for a certain number of people, but increase that number and you reduce the duration of the oxygen. On the other hand, as soon as this oxygen is released and circulating with all the rest of creation it will renew itself and there will be no limit to it. If we wish to formulate this philosophically, we may say that as soon as we include the limitless in our reckoning, we can tolerate and sustain a much more productive, much more complex structure of society; but as soon as we believe that the bee collecting nectar from the flower is taking it away from us, as soon as we believe that we can only live if we kill and destroy every other competing element of life, we are restricting our own lives, and eventually we shall be killing and destroying each other, because we shall believe that every man lives at the expense of every other.

This is not a valid philosophy, or rather, it is only valid in confined areas. For instance, if you are in a beleaguered fortress with only so much grain, you will know that there are so many meals and no more. But even in such circumstances there are elements to reckon with other than survival, and these are imponderable. We must learn that there may be other ways of escaping from a tight corner than that of blind resistance.

Last but not least, one of the most essential elements in life is humour, and the capacity to laugh at oneself, as at one another. This is an important ingredient in well-balanced human beings, or—as my little son used to say at three years old—'humour beings'.

BRISTOL, 1962

13. The Teaching of the Young

I FEEL something of an impostor in proposing to speak about the teaching of the young.[1] To the extent that the child has survived in me for some fifty years and that, notwithstanding, I may have gained some perspective on the matter, I suppose I enjoy the same authority as, say, an old cab-horse might have in speaking about the training of cab-horses! As for the formal authority to speak on this subject that would derive from a lifetime's association with schools, first as a student, then as a teacher, I have absolutely none.

Particularly do I feel my own inadequacy within so mature a civilization as the British, which has given the world such high proof of its concern for and success with the teaching of the young.

Perhaps this success lies partly in this people's reluctance to define too arbitrarily, or to be content with abstractions. This fundamental identification with the feeling rather than with its abstraction has led to the enrichment of language, to the search for ever finer, subtler inflections of meaning, to the humane and compassionate capacity of feeling for and with every human state of being: witness the myriad words for every kind and every degree of pain, which certainly do not exist in other Romance or Germanic languages. Other countries know only the signs for STOP and GO: here one finds road-signs reading YIELD and GIVE WAY. (But the Eskimos have, I believe, about half a hundred words for the different aspects of ice!)

The fundamental distrust of large, sweeping assumptions, of untried hypotheses, has saved 'this happy breed' from many con-

[1] The Campbell-Orde Memorial Lecture, delivered at the Golden Lane Theatre, London E.C.1, under the auspices of the Arts Educational Trust, on 25 November 1970.

temporary aberrations in the fields of psychology, sociology, politics and education.

Surely a very few words are worse than none, for the variety of action and sensation is lost in the paucity of words. For instance, the words 'housing', 'space' and 'cost' have usurped the whole gamut of words describing human shelter. The qualifying adjectives used are 'prestige' or 'council'. The hearth and the home have been reduced to cost per cubic foot. There is a crying need for cities, streets and houses to reflect the imagination, the vision of a society. Today we are fortunate in having the widest possible command over the greatest variety of materials and techniques, beyond the dreams of our forebears, and yet we are making very little use of these in terms of that aesthetic environment which might exist. Perhaps the most dangerous words of all are the two which, in the absence of further elucidation, take on a brutal finality—the words 'good' and 'bad'. But how many architects or tenants today can discuss such basic matters as exposure to sunlight, heat, cold and wind; or the shape or atmosphere of a room, or its acoustics, both internal and external? There are few in whom knowledge and instinct are so wedded as to give them that absolutely sure touch, that infallible sense of choice. The single word may so easily become the package bereft of original content and, as nature abhors a vacuum, emotional or otherwise, a new synthetic content is substituted.

My only title to speaking about the teaching of the young rests in the pragmatic experience of a lifetime of errors and trials —I say this advisedly, for in every case I made the error first— in learning, self-teaching and the imparting of my ideas to colleagues, young and old, and the gradual distillation of a few convictions and approaches which, I feel, tend to reduce the error.

One of these is that teaching is the giving of life, as un- predictable in its further living repercussions as life itself. This prolonged act of giving depends on a fusion of assurance and humility, as also on the reciprocated satisfaction of the student, and is in itself the condition of the teacher's survival.

It is unlike training, which produces predictable results, for teaching is a preparation for independence of thought, of behaviour; it is the readiness to educate an equal who may in fact turn out to be a superior. It is the desire to create the superior, even to be hurt by him—as the fencing master might be by his well-taught pupil; it is this selfless, yet selfish desire and need which is the very life-blood of a teacher. Good teaching must, in fact, contain the possibility of dual rebellion, as much against one's own prejudices as a teacher as from that sharp pupil who may have detected a flaw in your argument before you yourself.

Books and words are useful accessories, but the word itself cannot convey what the thought and the emotion do not, and where these are at odds with the word, it is the feeling and not the word which is conveyed. When the mother says to the child 'Don't be afraid', the child will at once detect any fear in her voice, and if fear is there the admonition will be useless.

The artist is aware of this phenomenon of communication, for he knows that 'words without thoughts never to heaven go'. In fact, the teaching of music, dance, drama and mime—the arts which are as demanding of the body as they are of the spirit— provide us with the clue to the whole teaching process, the process of integrated discipline and liberation, two concepts which are complementary and essential to each other, but which become mutually exclusive and independently explosive when education, which is the union of the two, has failed.

Concentration, a state of being wherein our totality is focused upon one intent, is automatic in a child. The child has a natural sense of mystery, of concentration, and of respect for what it wants to learn, for the learning process. The playing of games and the learning process are one with the child, and provided he is given what he longs for, he is full of gratitude. Have you ever seen the concentration on a child's face as he sits looking at a spider weaving his web? Today I could sit for hours looking at this, and in fact one of my greatest regrets is that I have never seen a spider's web woven from the first thread to the last. I have seen a spider catch his prey, however.

As adults we delight in the satisfactions of a child, for they are total. Soon the ear and then the eye provide signs which stand for the first total sensations, which require a choosing of inter- pretations, but which are already symbols replacing the primary experience. The progression is from tactile feel to sound, then to sight—and finally to concepts that are purely cerebral. My feeling is that when this order is reversed in the child's education, i.e for instance when the intellectual abstraction occurs too soon, or independently of a living equilibrium established between the environment and the child, a problematic situation ensues, requiring the regeneration of atrophied faculties.

Education has various elements: the oldest and most effective are example, opportunity and satisfaction, as a bird might show its young how to fly. At this level the direct and oral is paramount. A book, or any object causing a deviation of attention from parent or teacher, is not only superfluous, but harmful. At its highest levels this is the Socratic method, as practised in the best schools in Britain, in which the source of knowledge and stimulus is the live human being, not the dead book.

After the example stage we have the artificial ones—factual, analytical, abstract—but these should always be built gradually upon the living-example method. Where example and the satisfaction of opportunity fulfilled are in short supply, overworking of the further stages leads to false premises, conclusions and behaviour.

To begin with the child must learn a great deal orally—stories, melodies, rhythms and poetry, to which it reacts and which it finally recites or sings. The child should *make* a lot of things with its hands, and have the satisfaction of accomplishing something beautiful, something finished—making a pair of shoes, making primitive musical instruments, blowing glass, painting, drawing, carpentry. These activities are extremely important in an age where the factory has usurped the workshop, and it is more than ever vital to re-teach the craft and to give the possibility of complete expression to an individual's hands and fingers, to his mind and to his imagination. The child should express its totality in activity—singing, dancing, painting—and in repose before it develops any separate specializations. The imaginative must precede the factual and be disciplined by the reality of the factual, coming to grips with the hard, intractable, basic material while serving a vision.

I feel that with children one should as far as possible begin at beginnings rather than at ends. In other words, with the raw materials, with questions rather than with answers. For instance, one might postulate to the child the idea of the night sky seen year in year out by shepherds tending their flocks, beginning the study of astronomy on the basis of the possible observations which such a shepherd might have made in the course of his lifetime, and to speculate on the number of shepherds' lifetimes that would be required to establish the first knowledge of the orbits of the stars.

I have frequently found more pleasure in reading earlier books —seventeenth- and eighteenth-century books on botany, biology and travel with their often beautiful drawings—than later ones. I would begin such studies with these older reports rather than with the drier, more scientific as it were, more accurate perhaps, revelations of the modern laboratory and microscope.

Even the mistakes of first observation have their interest and might be very salutary in teaching the brighter pupil, who may be on his way to becoming a scientist, that humility so strangely lacking in the teacher's own putative profession. How often, I wonder, should the teacher teach the child, the student, to suspend belief, particularly belief in the teacher's own and the child's own conviction? How often is it necessary to check on one's own beliefs and to purge them of the inevitable prejudice that creeps in? How often does the teacher persuade the child not to accept anything simply on authority, but to be ready to prove the thesis, the assumption from the very beginning?

Then again, teaching cannot be separated from society, or from the background of the child and the family. You cannot suspend the living environment and teach only facts. By doing that you will only reap monsters. The terrible results we see today are often the results of the loss of those first years; years without music, without mother's singing, without the reciting of poems and stories.

The textbook is so often merely something designed to relieve the teacher from taking further initiative, or from any original thought. Perhaps a reduction of these teaching aids might raise the level of teachers. An Indian businessman I know in Madras comes to mind, and there are probably many others like him, who every day for one hour recites his oral heritage from the Bhagavad Gita. The little urchin raised by his six older brothers and sisters in one room has more of an environment than the lonely child raised in comfort.

The practising musician, especially the musician from birth, need never fear this atrophy if he has had the good fortune to love music at first hand from his mother's lullaby or, for example, as I did, from my father's very moving Chassidic songs: he will never disassociate the symbol from the act, he will maintain the relation, however tenuous, between the word and its primary meaning. Music is the bridge between the abstract and the tangible, between imagination and reality.

We have tended to restrict the concept of education to schools and classrooms, to books and words. It is because I have such a reverence for words and books, as I have for the score of a Beethoven Symphony, that I feel they deserve to be approached with a depth of feeling, a knowledge and memory of want and satisfaction, of anguish and pleasure, which they will reflect and sublimate. It is these, the primary sensations, born with life and in the family cradle, which spell not only the arts and crafts, but all those essential human and social services which, for instance, the American way of life is finding difficult to provide.

The student must feel gratitude and reverence for all knowledge acquired. We need nurses, teachers, policemen, as well as violinists and dancers.

Unfortunately school teaching is obliged to be corrective from the first years. To some degree it may attempt to remedy the defects of those homes which fail to provide the basis of daily hygiene, good posture, verbal expression, and so on, but how many of our young people are prepared for giving first aid, for looking after the first-born, or for that matter looking after themselves; or even have a knowledge of diet, or are aware of the particular dangers of our era in terms of disease and pollution? How many are educated to reject the vulgar, the one-dimensionally commercial, or have been alerted to the hollowness of propaganda? How many schools teach proper concentration or meditation, as the Jesuits and other religious orders do regularly? How many teach courage in defending others as well as ourselves, our principles and ideals? How many teach the cleansing of one's thoughts as well as one's body?

We must also teach and train *against* certain things, against the use of drugs and alcohol, against vulgarity and bad taste, against indulgence, against lack of compassion, against always believing the printed word; we must teach immunity to propaganda; and these lessons must be begun from the earliest age.

There is an old Jewish story of a father and his son going for a walk alongside a rather high wall. The little boy asks to be placed on top of the wall, so that he can walk along the narrow parapet. The father agrees but the boy makes him promise that he will catch him when he wants to jump down. Finally the boy, having walked a good while, asks the father if he may jump down. The father lets him jump, but does not catch him; the boy bruises himself rather severely and is terribly disappointed and angry with the father. Thereupon the father says, 'I just wanted you to learn. This is just to teach you never to trust anybody.' This is a somewhat exaggerated method, I would say, but it contains its grain of truth.

It is so important to choose non-habit-forming pleasures, which are not lethal, and which would replace the habit-forming ones. The child must be warned not against the policeman, who in Britain is still a friend, but against drug pedlars, 'pushers', and others of their ilk. Children must be taught and trained to debunk the god Mammon, and to treat him simply as the serviceable commodity that exchange and commerce provide—a convenience and nothing more. At least when I was a child the United States dollar was redeemable in gold at any bank; how I regret never having availed myself of that privilege! At least the paper was then a symbol of a real value. Today people worship paper, and all their values and pleasures are transitory for this reason. Dolls may be important as symbols in early childhood, but how depressing it is to see adults pursuing only phantoms, the station-wagon rather than the garden plot, the make-believe instead of the real. What a person really *is* has given way to what impression he makes. It is said that when Nixon was asked to what he attributed his electoral success he replied, 'To my make-up man.'

Sooner or later the real effect of situations—disease, war, tragedy, strife—reveal the person, and that real person is more likely to succumb or to commit suicide than to face up to the challenge if he has not been given the kind of teaching I am speaking about.

Basically, education must for these purposes be a guide to deep and lasting satisfactions, and must condition and train against instant satisfactions. One might say that gold, which of course gives no real satisfaction but is none the less a beautiful and useful metal, has given way to the drug, the 'instant' satisfaction of which paper money is the essential symbol. Real satisfactions must be provided in terms of love, reward, pride—real enjoyment of long-awaited pleasures and fulfilments.

I can still remember my first beer in the mountains of Sinaia in Rumania when I was eleven; my first taste of wine; my first taste of champagne—given to me by an understanding mother who knew the symbolic value to a boy of champagne at eleven o'clock in the morning.

With very young seedlings we exercise the greatest care; with young horses and dogs as yet not battery-reared (sport has its very real uses) we take every care, but we submit our children to the most haphazard and indiscriminate upbringing, and we wonder at the skinheads, the apathetic, the morbid, and the violent. Children are among the most defenceless creatures, and from their very infancy they are now fed with the crudest, the most vulgar, and the most violent material.

In fact, I feel that the younger generation is not only far better than we deserve, but that the overwhelming majority are evolving a relative sense of values that is less commercial than ours, and more aware of a total living economy in terms of fellow-creatures and of all life on land and sea, less violent through default though perhaps more violent through intent, and more realistic in terms of the need for a shift of direction, a shift of emphasis.

But will those many who have missed out on the early years ever make up for lost time and become trustworthy leaders and protectors of subsequent generations?

We at the Yehudi Menuhin School and the Arts Educational Trust are constantly reminded of that spinning wheel of the generations which, like our earth, depends upon the readiness of one generation to give its strength, its motion, its support, in fact its very life to the next round.

Peter and Margaret Norris, who have taught at the School since the very beginning, have recently provided it with its youngest member. Little Anthony has attended more rehearsals, classes and concerts than many another a hundred times his age. I am infinitely grateful to Providence for having denied my parents the wherewithal to leave me at home with a baby-sitter at the age of two instead of dragging me to orchestral concerts. My first recollection of violins is from the terrifying height of the highest gallery, nestled in my mother's arms. Even the child left to care alone for his six younger brothers and sisters, even the child working away at his carpenter's bench at the age of four, or practising the violin, is more fortunate than his contemporaries who grow without vision or responsibilities. Remember that the more that is expected of children in the time of their own development the more grateful they are.

Just as the basic moral precepts have only developed but never changed, so has the human ideal remained constant. Let me be so pedantic as to list the qualities society should encourage: self-reliance, flexibility, trustworthiness, loyalty, compassion, aesthetic intuition, health, lack of prejudice, the capacity for taking responsibility and for giving encouragement, imagination, creativity, a philosophical attitude, enthusiasm, inventiveness, longevity, the ability to be a source of comfort, courage and support to one's family and society, faithfulness, mastery of self, of a craft and of a subject, open-mindedness, political maturity, ability to teach—a person with such qualities would also be a world citizen, yet true to his home roots.

Should we not take stock and consider what elements in our total environment contribute to further these ideals? Just as economy can no longer be considered in its narrowest, most immediate sense of monetary profit or loss, but must include the totality of all life and life's future, so must education no longer mean one path only but must include every influence and every ideal. I do not mean *total control*, or total *laisser faire*. I mean total awareness, inspiration and dedication. I mean a stronger *ethos* and fewer laws and regulations.

Our mind, our brain, nature's computer, works almost instantly and has created abstractions to handle realities and processes. The time-lag between the word and the deed may be very great either way. The word (which stands for the deed) is indeed magic if it can conjure its own particular reality. Words without thoughts or deeds, goods without meaning and need, the illusion of instantaneous satisfactions and deeds divorced from preparation as from consequences, the false magic of empty words and devalued money—these represent the false religion which we must combat as superstitions, as ritualistic as any tribal practices and beliefs in our forbears.

Our aim must be not to force literacy down the throats of the people, but rather to restore the illiterate, be he tramp, gipsy, craftsman, or labourer, to a position of social importance, usefulness and service. If, after mastering a craft, a human being (child or adult) feels the compulsion to learn the more abstract symbols of written language, he or she must by all means be satisfied. We should then see a great resurgence of spiritual and aesthetic fertility.

We must oppose all uniformity of approach, all standardization, all blind faith in the one and only. Now that we have moved from the multiform pagan to the uniform God, we must find the true balance in a Pantheon of lesser deities, fructifying and competing with each other.

As applied to schools this principle would demand the widest possible diversity of schools and schooling. The need for all types of school is greater than before, particularly for the earliest kindergarten, and for the boarding school. The nursery room has disappeared from the new dwelling. The complete atmosphere of an integrated cosmos as it should exist for the growing child has vanished from urban society. It must now be replaced somehow at every level of education: perhaps this may be easier in the boarding school, just as knowledge was sheltered in the Dark Ages in the monasteries of old.

LONDON, 1970

14. A Musical Education

A MUSICAL EDUCATION is unlike any other: it was no coincidence that Einstein played the violin, for 'time', as a fourth dimension, is no mere abstraction to a musician, but rather an infinite living, pulsating continuum, varied and mobile, sometimes dense, sometimes weightless, sometimes eruptive, sometimes still, its laws identical with those interacting ones of gravity, speed and weight which govern spatial phenomena. No wonder the ancient Greeks found music in the heavenly spheres. I wish I knew enough about science and astronomy to relate accurately, for instance, intervallic proportions and their mutual attractions and repulsions, or overtone progressions, to their spatial counterparts.

The fantastic thing about music is its ability to reflect every conceivable occurrence and situation, whether animate or inanimate, whether an infant's cry or the sound of thunder, whether the travails of love as in a Schubert song, or of intellect as in a Bach fugue. The very quality of sound is akin to touch, and it is, in fact, verbally described as warm, cold, silken, velvety, sensuous, or dry.

How extraordinary is the paradox that music is once removed from reality, reality reinterpreted and reflected in the apparently intangible dimension of sound, and yet can be as immediate as a slap in the face and as voluptuous and erotic as the act of love. It can also be cold, clinical and calculating.

Above all, music is a wonderful master and mentor. For one thing, we cannot overshout it: we must listen, as in itself it is a pure exercise—sublimating other and cruder urges to concretize. Therein may also be its dangerous side, for it offers a ready escape from reality. I for one believe that the musician should constantly renew and retravel the paths between a full experience of living and his isolated private Muse, for otherwise she—his inspiration, his driving power—will wither.

Who better than a musician can span the range between the silent and the strident, between the still small voice—the softest sound we know, inaudible to everyone else, and yet the most compelling—and the overwhelming crash of destruction and (perhaps) resurrection?

And what of sound itself, the supreme element in communication, the uninterrupted and continuous apprehending of our environment which the aural gift ensures? It is the vibrations of sound that gave birth to words, to messages of every description, and even as we read these words silently with our eyes, we are in fact listening to their remembered sound with our inner ear. Sound is indeed the supreme medium of communication, and how much more significance do words hold when they are restored to sound, in the voice of our beloved, or in that of a great actor or statesman, a teacher, or even an Army sergeant major!

It is the music in the words which actually lends them meaning; it is the music in our intellect, as well as in our hearts, which spells the capital difference between the dead hand of the vacant printed symbol and the living resonant communication of concept, intent, and feeling. How important to the infant are the first voices and the quality they impart, for during an entire lifetime those words will carry the resonance, the quality and meaning they first possessed. Far more numerous than the words we write or even read are the words we think and dream, filling our inner ear and mind with an almost continuous Babel—that private and privately audible world which memory, thought and dreams inhabit and which to our conscious existence is an unending torrent of words. What a difference it must make how these myriad words sound to each of us, for we human beings spend the greater part of our days and nights with them. And how blessed the poet and the musician who can escape this verbal invasion by returning to pure sound and metre and by restoring the word to its original medium and dimension. For surely the first word was *sound*, and when we read in St John 'In the beginning was the word', we must hear music, for God is music and music is God, and as voice and words are nothing but breath, was not 'breath upon the waters' perhaps the first word?

When people speak, it is as important to listen to the music they are making (and sometimes it is pretty poor), as it is to the words they have chosen. Sometimes it is important to forget words altogether and let music take over, as we do when we listen to a Beethoven quartet. This reminds me of how these very Beethoven quartets once saved the life of a remarkable woman, now in her eighties, still happy and buoyant: she is the mother of Antal Dorati, the conductor. It was at the end of the war when the Germans were rounding up the Jews in Budapest and she found herself herded into a small room with dozens of others, where they were kept for many days with no food and no facilities of any kind. Most of the others went out of their minds, but she kept sane by methodically going through the four parts of each of the Beethoven quartets, which she knew individually by heart.

Such an experience testifies to what I would call a real education and, by the same token of course, a musical education. A real education is one which, in itself valuable, also infuses our every act, gesture and thought in the same way that music permeates our whole being. As I suggested that the 'word' and the 'breath' are synonymous with Creation, and as singing comes closest to uniting the two, I would say, therefore, that this education I speak of begins with singing, as it does in the choir schools and in the State schools in Hungary, where the Kodály method is in use. Perhaps the children graduating from these schools in Hungary will be no different from the prospective naval cadet interviewed by an Admiral friend of mine, who was interested in the young man's character and general knowledge. He usually introduced a musical question into the interrogation, and in this case he asked the applicant: 'Name me one of the greatest composers.' Stammering, stuttering, embarrassed and awkward, the young boy finally muttered 'FRAUST!' Needless to say he passed.

However, it is established beyond doubt from an exhaustive official report entitled 'Music Education in Hungary', that the children beginning each day with one hour's choral singing, rhythmic exercises, musical notation, although no more gifted than other children, are nevertheless substantially more alert intellectually, greatly superior in abstract thinking, in co-ordination, in spatial relationships, in good health, in the use of time, in initiative, in imagination, in the use of words and in good taste than their contemporaries who as yet have not been included in the music education programme. I have invited one of Zoltan Kodály's most experienced collaborators to come to England for two years to introduce this method to the children at my School, as well as to various schools of the Greater London Council.

Of course, although the Hungarian method derives from their own ancient folk material collected and organized by Bartók and Kodály, and the chants and songs are the product of these, their greatest composers, there is every incentive to the greatest composers in every country to produce suitably graded material, beautiful and inspiring, which would suit the temperament of their respective peoples.

What better understanding of another people can we have than through their music? Nothing has revealed the Negro soul in its nostalgic, noble sadness—long before the torrent of words or dissertations by sociologists and psychologists—more than the Negro Spiritual, nor their tribal society and collective abandon, than their percussion.

What key could unlock more completely the devout and spiritual, the symbolic and exalted world of Bach than his cantatas? Can anyone penetrate the solitary, mystic search of the Indian more deeply than through the improvisation of Ravi Shankar, or understand more completely the inexorable pulse of the Hindu than through the tabla beats of Alla Rakha?

You will understand that for me 'a musical education' is one in which life itself unrolls as might a great work of music. It is not limited to teaching children to play or sing, and must so infuse their lives that they live a song, as it were. To summarize what music is, I would like to quote a short passage that I wrote a few months ago: 'Music creates order out of chaos; for rhythm imposes unanimity upon the divergent, melody imposes continuity upon the disjointed, and harmony imposes compatibility upon the incongruous. And as confusion surrenders to order and noise to music, and as we through music attain that greater universal order which rests upon fundamental relationships of geometrical and mathematical proportion, direction is supplied to mere repetitious time, power to the multiplication of elements, and purpose to random association.'

LONDON, 1966

15. If I were Eighteen

IF I WERE EIGHTEEN I would, of course, like to have the best of both worlds. I would want the experience that comes with years, *and* youth—like having both wealth and the knowledge of how to spend it wisely—as the French say, 'si jeunesse savait, si vieillesse pouvait'. Yet I will try to be realistic and speak only of what I feel and am convinced should be within the grasp of a person of eighteen.

At a time when life is mainly before us, as at sunrise, when we have the whole day ahead; when finally unprotected we are cast upon the elements, when at our own risk we must establish an independent relationship with the earth, at this time we should want to know everything that might help establish a harmonious working relationship with our environment, as well as everything that might make our myriad choices more certain. We should want to know everything that might save those around us, as well as ourselves, from pain and loss of time.

It is difficult for the person of eighteen to realize that his or her days are numbered, and yet the same laws of economy obtain in life as in science, mechanics or business. By the time I was eighteen I had worked at music and my violin for over twelve years. This was a gain in time. On the debit side there were many relationships, much experience and wisdom, which I should have known by the time I was eighteen, and in which I was far behind. We must for ever work to prepare the morrow and the morrow's morrow; just as we must prepare during all our young years for a happy and healthy old age, so we must prepare during our whole lifetime for a quiet and happy death, not by concentrating upon it, but by cultivating the faith which assures us that, coming at its proper time, it will be as welcome as marriage for the twenty-year-olds.

Unlike primitive human societies, in which all man's functions and all the major milestones of life and death are pre-ordained and predetermined by severe tradition, taboo and habit, our fields of endeavour are bewilderingly many, our choices of good and bad almost unlimited, and the dangers correspondingly greater.

As we grow up we are taught subjects, crafts and trades, but we are not taught survival. The result is that many young people reach the age of eighteen without knowledge of their historical, psychological, physiological, geographical or cultural background, nor with an understanding or knowledge of how to live.

For example: how many young people have good habits of hygiene, or know the proper use of the elements around us and which actually constitute us? How many know how to breathe and move, how to put the body though its paces every morning? The use of water? Breathing and posture? Proper nutrition? How many of our urban population in America today, or even of our farming population, are acquainted with the night sky and the great constellations? How many have a clear idea about our relationship to and dependence upon the earth, our responsibility to ourselves and our children and our children's children? For we must realize that we cannot take out of anything more than we put into it if we wish continuity of existence, nor can we always take out in one form and put in in another. Particularly must we respect the cycle of life, which if interrupted at any point by the substitution of a synthetic or inert substance for a living one, inevitably breaks down, bringing disease and death to all living things.

How many young students think that the human history of the United States began with the first European invasion? How many study the lore of the Indian civilizations which preceded the present? Those peoples at least preserved their heritage and bequeathed us a virgin country, bursting with fertility, with rich pastures, clear unpolluted rivers, great forests and enormous quantities of wild life. Look what has now been done to it with its dust-bowls, muddy, reeking rivers, the poverty of its wild-life, the destruction of most of its forests and the pollution of its air.

How many have penetrated and studied the contribution of the African, the West Indian and the American Negro to our own civilization, in music, in sport, and in many other fields? In fact how many have considered what a tremendous unseen and indirect influence the Negro has had upon our way of life? If we ourselves are good-natured, generous and kind, it is in no small measure due to the deep permeating of our entire way of thinking, feeling, acting, and speaking, and of our very physique, that is the result of centuries of contiguous habitation with this warm-hearted and still partly childlike race. As a nation too, if we love gay colours and have sensual qualities, these may be from the African influence; if we are God-fearing and proud it is probably from the English Puritans; if we are hard-working and methodical, perhaps too inclined to dot our i's and cross our t's, it is from the German contribution, and if there is any attachment to our soil it is probably from our Scandinavian heritage. If we love singing and music it is both the Italian and the German—and so do we for ever interweave the various strands which constitute the fabric of our nation.

If I were eighteen today and were interested in medicine I would think of the numerous hospital patients we have every year and would want above all to do something about preventive medicine. If we knew as much about preventive medicine as we do about surgery, which deals mainly with the removal of an already diseased part, there would be far fewer people in hospital.

If I were eighteen today and loved the earth and Nature, I would work to redeem a bit of land, at first perhaps just a small piece, and then an ever larger one until, together with others, I had restored our land to fertility.

If I were eighteen and had a social conscience I would try to balance mass terms of reference with individual terms of reference, regardless of any formal or arbitrary classification of the individual.

If I were eighteen and had an historical bent I would search the parallels to our present problems in the long past, and thus the possible causes of our own difficulties; I would try to fathom the great, often inevitable world developments, which are behind the more superficial reports that circulate. Unfortunately, mankind often moves in blind reaction. I would try to get acquainted with other civilizations, not only by studying history and archaeology, but by travelling, preferably on foot, and talking my way through the world's villages. In my contacts with other countries I would seek to serve their children, and I would try to study every smallest thing which might reveal a new angle of approach, a new attitude to life, a new philosophy of values; I would try to learn in every oldest corner of this earth, and approach every living thing with humility and respect. Whatever I felt was wrong I would want to improve and change: it is right that youth should feel an intense ardour, a deep indignation, and that it should be ready for high inspiration and purpose. May these never be selfish and cruel, for it is so easy to mislead the human mind into thinking that it is fighting for something worth-while when it is actually only following its lowest instincts. Mass movements are dangerous, and I would avoid them. We lose our integrity, our balance of mind and all that humanity and mankind should strive for as soon as we have surrendered our soul to a mass. This I would always fight against.

I would hope by the time I was eighteen to see my parents and grandparents in a warm, loving light and yet objectively. Those faults and weaknesses which may be our burden by virtue of habit and heredity we must take full responsibility for ourselves, as we must be grateful for the advantages, strengths and opportunities which have been given us. It is important to be both mentally and emotionally disentangled, and yet to recognize the indissoluble bond which must express itself in devotion and love.

I would certainly be in love and dedicated to something. I would also remember that only when one is ready to sacrifice oneself in defence of something is it possible to receive like treatment when in need of love, help and respect for oneself.

One cannot think of the age of eighteen without thinking of the relationship between boys and girls. Is one at that time in love with one or with many? It is possible to remain faithful to one idea and to its symbol, even to a person, so long as the idea remains unrealized and unincorporated. This pure idealization should, if possible, be prolonged. Once an attachment is consummated, however, a repeatable sequence takes shape, which then exists in its own right. At that point one may often become confused, unable to decide between the two principles of the one and of the many. Is one at this stage a roving bull or a wide-eyed cow (as the case may be), or is one still a human being with all one's infinite capacity for single-mindedness, concentration, power of focus, exclusive devotion—as for instance in dedication to, belief and trust in a supreme being?

We must remember that the human race itself has proceeded conceptually from the many to the one: from numerous and multiple gods to the one supreme symbol, whether utterly nameless or as revealed through human life. The single human life, if given a chance to mature, also evolves along similar lines.

We must also remember that in the animal kingdom there are examples of unique and utter devotion, as for instance the Great Swan, which follows its single mate in death. The human being learns also, sooner or later, that the most precious values in life, the fruits, the dividends, the rewards, as well as the joys for ourselves and society, are those which accumulate, which continue unbroken and which, like a great tree, dig their strong roots ever deeper and spread their sheltering foliage ever higher. Cut flowers die quickly.

In this age of great choice and corresponding confusion it is necessary to ponder a little longer—to know oneself better, to take sufficient time so that one may recognize in another a little more clearly those qualities which will contribute in the years ahead to the fullness, the solidity and the strength of the joint living edifice.

If I were eighteen I would take full advantage of the privilege of my age to question every ready-made opinion, and refuse to accept anything for true that I had not convinced myself was actually so. A few basic convictions are better than many an uncertain and ill-founded opinion.

I should not be ashamed to say 'everyone seems to know, but I have not yet made up my mind'; or 'I am not sufficiently informed to have an opinion.' Real life should not consist of ready-made railings which we grab at and cling to with panic-stricken intensity, fearing that we may otherwise fall without support into the yawning abyss. These symbolize our prejudices—ready-made railings are the equivalent of ready-made opinions. Real life consists in finding anew at every moment that perfect sense of equilibrium which demands a delicate sense of poise, much as the tightrope-walker who despite the risks is actually safer on his feet than some poor crippled arthritic holding on to his crutches for dear life. 1959

16. *Art and Science as Related Concepts*

An attempt at their comparative anatomy as revealed
in various fields of human endeavour

THE RELATIONSHIP between science and art is a very deep
and important one and is similar in function to the very legs
we stand and move on. These must be both independent of each
other, and at the same time in harmony and in synchronization.
Science and art function quite naturally and perfectly in any
simple act, whether it be a kind word or whether a surgeon is
operating on living tissue. The creative act is as much a part of
science as it is of art and as it must be of every living gesture.

It is only a pity that this automatic association, which is largely
subconscious, has suffered: we have allotted a sealed compartment
to each, and since the day when consciousness was awakened by
the eating of the apple of knowledge we have injured that unity
and harmony which characterize man's image of the perfect past,
and its counterpart the perfect future—the Garden of Eden and
Heaven—where undoubtedly art and science were and will always
be one. Our lives exist, however, for the most part in this miserable present, between the other two which we shall never know
except as 'present'!

I conceive of art as the organization of a living moment and
science as the crystallization of an eternal truth. I see art as
predominantly the intuitive, the 'feminine', and science as
predominantly the deliberate and 'masculine' element.

One of the chief distinctions to which I shall return is that
science is predictable and art is unpredictable. The living moment
is unpredictable, and therein lies one of the chief confusions
of our day. We would impose the measuring rod on the
immeasurable.

We have lost the sense of the continuous in the cycle of life,
which belongs to the intuitive half, and as a result, we attempt

cruelly and hopelessly to subject the living and life itself to the rules and principles of the utterly predictable. Life then eludes us and revolts, for it will not be dominated in this way. (We saw how in one of the most civilized nations of the world, and in the name of principle, life was debased to soap and lampshades.) The predictable has wrought great changes in our lives, and because the applied principles of science, together with an immense technique, have brought us in great measure power, control, transportation, comfort and security in isolated spheres, we have idolized the application, mistaking the refrigerator and the tractor for the theorem.

In Leonardo da Vinci or Michelangelo's day art and science, to a high degree, were often incorporated in the same person, as indeed they must always be in their pure state. The washing machine and the aeroplane were still only wishes or exploratory drawings, and the Mona Lisa and David were supremely unique. Applied science and applied art had not yet succeeded in stamping out a million duplicates of each.

Man for ever craves uniqueness as his birthright, as a snowflake or a fingerprint—each one different. He wants to, and indeed he must also consciously exist in the unpredictable, in the creative and intuitive moment, a moment which in that particular way has never happened, nor will ever happen again.

I would like to describe what I feel about intuition. It is a particular form of knowledge, just as steam is a particular embodiment of water, or vice versa. On the one hand we have instinct, the legacy of our efforts at survival, consisting of habitual conditioned responses both acquired in our lifetime and inherited from the thousands of generations that preceded us. It is an accumulation of data correlated to the ensemble of our sensing, feeling and thinking processes—data so vast in their scope and detail as to be utterly beyond the capacity of the best human brain deliberately to reconstruct and co-ordinate. This would be but like the slow sifting of judicial evidence or adding and subtracting with children's blocks, compared with the electronic calculating machine.

I would say that on the other hand intuition embraces a further dimension as well—perhaps the most important one. This includes the unspecified ideal, the magnet, the light towards which mankind's evolution and nature's developments infallibly lead, and which *precedes* and is the condition of this evolution and development. To the extent that continuity is associated with an irreversible process we are being continually guided to an end. In this sense intuition is certainly aware of a direction, and to that extent of predictability. This dimension exists in the smallest particle of matter, but escapes analysis and explanation on the basis of the materialist dogma of action and reaction. I would place the aesthetic and the moral (another form of aesthetic) in this category. How else could such things exist, from the plumage of birds to the trees which grow to heaven, or to the greatness of drama?

As there are two sides to the cycle (one of which is the absorption of light by matter and its transformation into energy, which can serve as a description of life, a function which can only be achieved by living matter, including our fossilized fuels, coal and oil, which again are and can only be the reduction over millions of years of vegetable and marine animal life, and the other the transformation of the energy into light, which is what we receive from the sun), the universe is at all times and at all places evolving in some irreversible direction, of which we may be instinctively or intuitively aware, however delicately poised we may be at any given moment between the two poles of light and matter, heaven and hell, or past and future. We are at all moments part and parcel of complementary irreversible processes, which are carrying us simultaneously to our doom and to our redemption or release. We may to a certain extent choose.

To resume: intuition is the condensation of all experience, as it is the awareness of eternity and infinity, of duality within unity, of the cycle of life, of matter and of all occurrences.

I would like to make quite clear that in speaking of instinct or intuition I by no means refer to something or to some urge which escapes cultivation, discipline or refinement. On the contrary. The highest levels of intuition in life and in art can only occur when the mind and the emotions are pure, dedicated and untarnished, and when the technique of expression and thought has reached a high stage of automatic control and freedom. This is the process of a deliberately acquired technique becoming instinctive.

Instincts and hungers which no longer serve us destroy us. We seek their appeasement and satisfaction, with no relation to the requirements they serve, as with greed for food, or intense and crude emotions such as are aroused and appeased vicariously in a cinema, the satisfaction of which can be bought for cash and without any real participation. In this way we lose the feeling of unity with our background and we seem quite content to burn up nature's and mankind's resources of air, water, soil, fish, fowl and forests without compassion or compunction. We forget too easily what these represented to our forebears and must still mean to our own life and future; we lose the flavour and the capacity for our own ecstasy, love, fear and beauty. Provided these emotions, intrinsic to man's life, can be served up synthetically, and can trigger off our conditioned reflexes at preordained hours, as it were, we seem quite content.

In the light of the great achievements which mark the evolution of life in general and man in particular, milestones in philosophy, biology, art, and so on, as against the relatively recent application of full consciousness and objectivity in science, which has brought such rich rewards (although not perceptibly so in mass ethics and morals) it seems ludicrous that today it is necessary to assert that the intuitive is capable of as great and of parallel 'discoveries', results, effect, and achievements as the scientific. The difference is that the intuitive results are secured from within ourselves and in fact by the observance of the same principles and disciplines as we hold to in the laboratory, namely: precision, economy, singleness of purpose, open-mindedness, dedication, absence of prejudice, humility. These disciplines are turned inwards, instead of (as in science) outwards.

I would like to propose two axioms as the pinions of my theory.

No. 1. *No phenomenon or sensation discovered, contrived or executed by science is possible unless its equivalent has already existed in nature.* This applies as well to those achievements which are self-evident, as flying (birds), and the production of energy or light from matter (sunlight), as for those less apparent (merely because of the fact that the vast majority of us contain untold and infinite potential faculties of which we are unaware), as wireless (telepathy) and others. It should be self-evident that man can only discover what already exists—except that with intuition and science he can juggle and reorganize, re-create, his component parts into ordered and serviceable patterns expressive of and subservient to himself—in art, in life and in science.

No. 2. *None of the basic revelations of what we like to call science are beyond the capacity of the single intuitive intellect to formulate in the comparative isolation of meditation.* Indeed, the intuitive conception precedes all realizations of applications. Whether it is the equation of matter with energy, or the corpuscular theory of matter, or the displacing of water by weight, or the rotation of the earth—these conceptions have been recorded thousands of years ago. In fact whether we think of some anonymous Hindu philosopher or of his 'reincarnation' Einstein, of Jesus (may his vision of brotherhood prevail some day), of Leonardo and his machines, of Archimedes or Pasteur, it is always the vision which comes first, and which appears as the result of the interaction of unprejudiced observation with intuitive understanding. Man has always meditated on the ultimate particle of matter, on the meaning of life; on eternity, infinity, fate and the duality of all phenomena.

Mankind's dark ages seem recurrent and perennial, prejudiced, brutal, arbitrary and abysmally ignorant (principally of what he has within himself), and having for the most part lost his innocence, and with it his intuition and nature's protection, and at the same time gaining little knowledge, man has time and again forfeited, perverted and abused his own dignity and his title to nobility. He has also betrayed the faith, hope, the clear commandments and the counsel which from time to time he received in the course of the millenia—from Lâot Tsze, Buddha, Moses, Spinoza, and in our own day from thinkers ranging from Brunner to Santayana.

While paying lip-service to these, indeed in their very name, always in the name of high principles and of that Almighty who has warned us not to use His name in vain, mankind has committed crime in every degree—crimes of omission as well as of commission. We have already paid in part for our own and for the others (as they are in a sense our own), and we will pay again as nations for that darkest lack of foresight of which we are even now guilty. We have been told and warned for thousands of years, 'Do unto others as you would they would do unto you.'

In other words to set the example. Noble example alone and not edict can guide and improve the human race. Would that we as individuals, as groups and as nations provided high examples of thought and conduct! How refreshing it is to find anywhere a forthright and selfless expression in action, of compassion or of indignation truly representative of a majority of the electorate!

I can hardly believe that we, here and everywhere, will escape those birth-pangs which may herald new life or complete destruction, which in our own generation and at this moment are being suffered by so many of our fellow-men—white, black, yellow, brown. And consider the gipsies, the Jews, the Poles—consider Hungary, Tibet, South Africa. (I do realize that the predictability of pain is one of the lowest forms which prophecy can take.)

The human being is in himself essential and complementary to the truth he discovers, as art is to science, and both are essential to create equilibrium at its highest, nor could his mind wrest the energy equations from the universe unless it were associated with intuition.

This confusion of the unpredictable and the predictable, of the living moment and its crystallization, is evident in most fields of endeavour, including such disparate activities as health, preventive medicine, diplomacy, education, administration, architecture, even town planning and others. All these involve actual life and the germinating processes, and are therefore too broad to be treated successfully by men or methods which would exclude the artistic and the intuitive. After all, architecture is more than engineering, neither do we expect the composition and the performance of music from musicologists, nor the painting of pictures by art critics!

Although I am not an authority in any of these fields, I would like to take up one or two of them, with some improvisational interludes in between, as in a fugue, to show the divergence of approach between the specialist on the one hand and the humanist (for want of a better word) on the other.

We are blessed in England, the United States and other countries, with parliamentary systems composed of executive, legislative and judiciary, each retaining its ultimate prerogatives beyond and above the dictates of experts or of any other self-styled authority. In other words, we place our trust in the intelligence, the ethics, and the morals of human beings who are expected, on the basis of a broad experience in life, of a disciplined schooling and of their knowledge and love of a common heritage in literature, art and history, to evaluate, draw conclusions, and take action on the basis of the facts they perceive, and which are brought to their attention. (At times their style may be somewhat cramped by periodically having to please an unenlightened or uninformed majority; at times their mistakes are merely the result of their own lack of wisdom.) Experts should be thought of as a prolongation of our senses, as the astronomer of our eyesight, the radar-crew of our ears, i.e., as purveyors of data, but they should never be allowed to be our mind, which must always reserve the right of ultimate decision. Although I have no knowledge of higher mathematics, nor can I build an engine, or even a simple chair, and although no-one today can make as good a violin as Stradivarius, or carve a more beautiful statue than could Praxiteles, I can nevertheless choose my furniture and arrange it, I can play a violin, I can understand the principles of nuclear fission, and I can glimpse the implications, physical and psychological, of nuclear energy.

FIRST THEME: THE FIELD OF MEDICINE

I would like to use cancer as an example of an ailment or condition which by its various definitions evokes in our mind analogous patterns in society, psychology and physiology. I would be so bold as to propose that the following thoughts deserve consideration even from the medical profession. I believe it is possible to describe cancer as follows: That which is normally a part of a whole and subservient to the requirements of that whole no longer recognizes its affiliation and declares itself independent and irresponsible; or expressed conversely, a whole unit loses its hold, its compelling sense of unity and purpose, allowing parts of itself to run rampant.

Already I have maintained that in great part, and particularly among our experts and their passive millions of worshippers, we have lost a sense of basic equations. Here again there is confusion between the living and the inert. May I propose two complementary axioms? (I use 'unspecified' in the following sense: that which cannot reproduce itself—or which is not a living part

Above: With Robert Masters, leader of the Menuhin Festival Orchestra

Below: Conducting the Menuhin Festival Orchestra

Above: Teaching at the Menuhin School, Stoke D'Abernon

Below: With Ravi Shankar

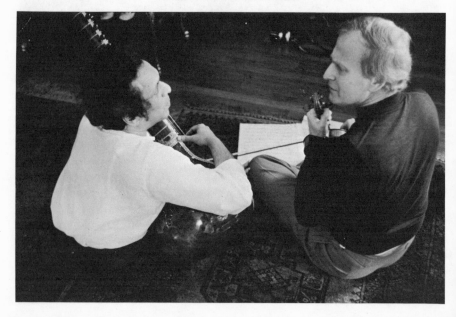

of an organism which can—in a specific living form of the vegetable or animal kingdom.)

No. 1. *Unspecified, anonymous fuel or food=unspecified anonymous growth* (in other words we can only expect what we put in). No. 2. *Specified, organic fuel or food=specified organic growth.* ('Organic' means related to and part of the whole.) Between Nos. 1 and 2 there is every degree. Let me explain.

Already we have seen how an instinct divorced from its *raison d'être* must become destructive. We have taken our two most pronounced taste guides, the sweet and the bitter, which in a natural diet infallibly guide us respectively to the richest nourishment in fuel (sugars) and minerals (salts), that is, which provide our motor and our structural requirements respectively, and we have reduced these to the parodies of refined white sugar and refined white salt; with our bleached and polished carbohydrates divorced from their germinating agents on the one hand and from their structural agents on the other. With this counterfeit currency we seek to still the age-old cravings of our bodies—with these utterly valueless, depraved and waste end-products we would maintain life and our bodies' will to live. Instead of welding our body as a whole into one harmonious instrument, which achieves its survival as a unit, moulded into compact shape by the endless hunt, the quest for sustenance, by the exercise and training of our faculties of choice, we provide it at every twist and turn, and with hardly any effort of its own, with fake fuel and fake structural material—soft drinks, candy bars, substances synthetic in appearance, flavour and consistency, as well as preservation. I would like our laboratories to take healthy animal tissue on the one hand, and a cancerous growth on the other, and see which of these thrives better on an exclusive diet of such denatured foods.

Of course certain carcinogenous substances cause or allow the actual initial revolt or basic breakdown of tissue, such as smoke for the lungs, coal tar, diesel oil for the skin and in our organs, and the poisonous chemical agents that we ingest in our food, water and air. Nevertheless, interesting statistics might be gathered, for instance by comparing the incidence of cancer in diabetics who must foreswear sugar, and others who eat it freely, or again between gymnasts who use their whole body, and others who, penguin-like, use it sparingly. Finally, the psychological implications of having a body not geared to use or accustomed to function as a unit, but of which each part may feel superfluous, swollen, incompetent and unsatisfied—these psychological implications and their physical counterparts should also be studied as they affect each other.

I cannot reconcile myself to the heavy burden and my possible guilt on seeing hundreds and thousands of people suffering unnecessarily (not only of cancer), while research in the abstract is buried in the isolated cancer cell, accumulating more and more data which, however fascinating and useful it will be, is mainly palliative and never preventive.

First interlude. It is ridiculous to see the halting approach of our peoples, tentative and insecure, to any problem not reduced by laboratory experiments to black and white. Such instruments as the violin, for instance, would never have been made and never played had humanity waited for a laboratory to decide on how to make and play a violin. No art, no language, no music, no medicine, and finally, no science, would have occurred if man had waited for scientific certainties. Certainly no children or poems would have seen the light of day if man and woman had insisted on knowing the theory first!

We must recognize the fact that as living human beings we are artists. Thus we must face our tasks in eager and humble expectancy, the challenges and the unpredictable with assurance and with faith, and at our best with an unfalteringly sure touch. As an artist I must make new and irreversible decisions at every moment, otherwise I am merely an identical printing machine, obeying the switch. Many of the troubles of our day can be set down to a certain arrogance of spirit and a corresponding lack of faith. I would say that so long as our approach relies preponderantly on the purely expert and scientific, so long it will falter and hesitate, so long it will be timid and insecure—or conversely, if assured, it may be arrogant and mistaken.

SECOND THEME: TOWN PLANNING

It has often struck me that certain architects must have understood the psychological, symbolic and physiological differences between the circular and the straight, the enclosed and the open: those who planned the Victorian squares and the Regency terraces of London; those who had the Napoleonic vision of the Etoile with its great arteries. The circular symbolizes the womb— intuitive, passive, productive, protective, mysterious, dark, personal. The straight line symbolizes the ideal, the path of light— the objective, the rational and the impersonal. And yet how often in practice is the intuitive direct and clear, and the rational confused and misleading!

When we use a straight line, as an avenue, we imply object and purpose, but a straight line, unless it resolves in a focal point, as is the case in Paris with the Arc de Triomphe, or the Louvre and the Place de la Concorde, is fraudulent, leading one by the nose to nowhere. For the actual connective tissue of a city, where people live and work and talk and rest, we must study the patterns of the branches of trees, each of which, though similar, is different. We must understand the convolutions of the brain, even of the intestine, and penetrate the dispositions of veins or the extraordinary patterns of finger-prints. In a leaf, just as in any organism, there is need for large and small arteries, for angles of every degree, and for backwaters free from any intrusion. Just as an organism has compartments in which it thinks, protected, and others where it acts, so must a city also. For the individual, a city must provide opportunities for circulation, social and community life in the proportion required. To conserve the unity of a town people must be able to face each other; they can hardly do so across the congested jumble of our busy streets or shoulder to shoulder. In the houses, within the blocks, they mostly turn their backs on each other. When they try to walk between each other's dwellings they are at the mercy of the befouled air, the onslaught of machines' noise and the elements in all their furies. In medieval towns, such as Rothenburg, there were narrow streets in which each house was set at a slightly oblique angle; in Renaissance towns, as in Bologna, there were arcades. Have we made any progress in urban living?

Our contemporary construction is of steel and concrete. Yet only now, after some sixty years, are the architects beginning to use more fully the advantages and characteristics inherent in these materials, which are the ability to apply the cantilever principle, and to build with free space, for air, light and sun, within the very body of the construction. We could today build a city that would be literally like the hanging gardens of Babylon, where pedestrians could walk at a high level between these gardens, leaving the lowest street level entirely for transport. Or ground floors could be wholly clear for pedestrian circulation and shopping in protective shelter. Within some districts no transport should be allowed, but only squares and gardens and, between these, larger and smaller arteries would connect and radiate as the larger and smaller branches of trees.

Why is the centre of Paris beautiful, and the centre of Indianapolis so ugly? Why are the grey tree-planted squares of London so satisfying and the Prussian-like Imperial alleys of workers' tenements the world over so soul-destroying (open at both ends, like digestive tracts—but lacking even a single restraining twist)?

Of course straight lines, as well as perfect circles and ovals, as in the crescents and the unified façades of the beautiful town of Bath, must be planned. On the other hand, the pulsating, vibrant city, in its convolution and evolution, should grow or be planned like the old towns, as does a tree—adapting itself at every moment to pressure, topography, functions, movements and seeds.

Also there is a natural proportion to be preserved between the straight line, representing the single ideal and direction, and the twisting trenches representing the infinite multitudes of events involved in living, as there is in a tree between the perfect, single, vertical direction and the myriad divergent and contributing angles, curves, widths and twists of its substance—roots, trunk, branches, leaves, bark and so on. Again we are speaking of the organic—of diversity within unity.

Second interlude. I would like to suggest that it is perhaps in Britain that my thesis can best be understood. There is no country that combines the artist and the scientist, inspiration and discipline, as does this country. There may be some which have pushed the one or the other to a higher degree (as the Germans have pushed discipline) but to raise both to an equal level and to enable each to complement the other means that the end-result is infinitely richer than could be any result based only on one leg, however long, and a crutch. The British love their flowers, their animals and their trees (though I dare say that if these could talk back they might be loved less). This intuitive sense explains the cult of eccentricity, which is so marked, despite the solemn, formal and conventional demeanour this country presents. What make of a person a unique individual are the marks and scars, the imprint of a particular personal experience, and the degree of reaction, of depth, in feeling, in thought, and in action that this experience has evoked. Life is our sculptor, and for better or worse we are hammered and chiselled into a particular shape; otherwise we remain lumps, without fluting, without capital or base. Also like a great artist, life ruthlessly destroys every work that is unsatisfying.

Art is the transmutation of a total effort, the transforming of one thing into another, in particular of pulse and sensation, of intuition and thought into acts, into sounds, sights, words, gestures, behaviour. It is the total expression of a given living moment recreated in ordered terms, terms which are an attempt to perpetuate the ephemeral, to capture for ourselves some infinitesimal part of eternity. It is the expression of the ideal, but not the predictable. How could it be predictable? How do we know when we begin a composition what details it will contain, or what a certain melodic twist will have tonight, tomorrow or at some other time?

There is, however, a great deal of science in art, and that is the ever-conscious, self-disciplined effort towards predictability. We try to eliminate everything which might tarnish or impede, prejudice, distort, or pervert the divine impulse (what the Germans call *die Heilige Einfalt*). We try to see to it that neither muscle, nerve, nor any of our organs, mind or heart may impede, but all must, like a well-trained team of horses, pull the coach along its path. We try every kind of exercise; we experiment with every conceivable line of attack, we explore every promising possibility which may provide a measure of control, and in its way we smooth the path for that wonderful, mysterious and unpredictable unknown. We polish the contact and verify the wiring so that all may be well to receive that faintest electric impulse, or perhaps that thunderbolt, when it comes.

This sounds like the pursuit of science, and that is what it is. It is the pursuit of predictability in art, just as the scientist at his highest moment is guided by the intuitive faculty of art. Science past its first flush of pride, and in the certainty of unilateral solutions to all problems (as it was naïvely believed that all problems in the past were problems of predictability), science holding the keys to predictability, firmly believed that it was bound to triumph over all and sundry, alone. Today science is more than ever bound to recognize and accept a permanent, however receding, dominion of mystery, which God is determined to keep to himself, and which may only be revealed in moments of inspiration, but which must be perpetually heeded and allowed for as the silent unpredictable witness (our conscience if you wish) of our waking hours. (Perhaps an ant, too, in its ceaseless toil, if at all aware, recognizes an infinite, *non*-receding area of permanent mystery. Or perhaps because the mystery is unyielding and static, it is not concerned with mystery at all.) We may be allowed to hope that man too—*each person*—will wake to a sense of his own uniqueness and irreplaceability, will realize the vessel he is and will recognize the one grain within him of mystery, of unpredictability, of God. If that could be so, a renaissance would follow from the assertion of the living, changing, moment of inspiration, from the respect for single blades of grass as emblems and stages in a cycle of life.

There is much to be learned in abandoning oneself to art or to science. It is the unremitting service of an ideal, and more can be learned in its practice than from any momentary or temporary act. For instance, just to draw a bow across the strings, as in playing an instrument, we learn economy of motion as well as the multitude and importance of each of the tiniest contributory motions required (as in a perfect drawing), the requirements which daily call forth faith, perseverance, devotion and love; we learn the evils of brutality, the aesthetic sharpening taught by economy and humility, the strength derived from weakness. There is a wonderful Chinese saying that youth and strength can be equated with flexibility, as in the young tree which bends to the winds, and age and death with rigidity. Strength is not always strength. The show of strength is very often weakness.

The control and direction of our emotions that science teaches us are in fact the basic equilibrium and the continuous alternating of opposing forces; darkness and light, circle and straight line, art and science, even inhaling and exhaling. We can extend the list almost indefinitely, as every quality finds its expression in the timing of a perfect gesture, or of an act.

Sometimes we learn from odd sources, as if by accident. In fact I would say that most of the *things* we learn come from sources we could not possibly predict. We learn that in a sense only the impossible (that which has never been possible or predictable before) is possible. We learn also how to rid the mind of unhelpful thoughts; we learn to build a healthy instinct, and what is very good, we learn to avoid the scapegoat mentality—for I alone am responsible for the sounds I make. We have perforce to learn to cultivate a sympathetic touch for people and things, and a respect for tools and crafts. We have to try to be honest in self-analysis, and in the fathoming of our own motives as they affect the quality and the capacity to do and to make.

One of the most important things we learn is the uselessness of frontal attack, and how the most successful assault is likely to be found along the undefended, uncluttered road. How important it is to create a climate free of the resistance of prejudice, or in the physical world, of muscle tension, which inhibits the formation of good habits. I have found out time and time again, how when a problem stands in the way it cannot be attacked as the problem it is, but only from every angle, from every devious angle—in other words it cannot be attacked as an unyielding impediment, but rather as something to be understood and dissolved, and the very effort of frontal attack inevitably defeats itself.

Then we learn another most important thing from our very motions, and that is to anticipate and to think ahead. It is important to pay for what we are going to get (even for what we receive as a gift), to pay in advance; it is important to anticipate, for it is always too late otherwise. It is a salient principle, and one which today is not sufficiently recognized. Neither the artist nor the farmer can afford to wait for the harvest before ploughing and tilling his land. It is the abstract element in our conception of life that is basically at fault, owing partly perhaps to the prevalance of buying, selling, and mortgaging in advance, and transferring this pattern of methods and habits to living processes. It cannot apply to living and to thinking. An artist must be deeply aware of cause and effect.

Artists are for ever wrestling with life, with human resistance and with the qualities and weaknesses of flesh, or with the world of crystallized certainties. I know that artists have been accused of building ivory towers, but I think that is one of the false suppositions of our day. The composers and the performers I know are very close to human beings, very close to the world, and they have to be if they want to express anything. They cannot draw and paint empty air, but must consume the realities about them. As artists we belong to that sophisticated breed that requires both the smells of the barnyard and the elaborate scents of Lanvin. All composers and painters, whether primitive, classical, or contemporary, testify to this, from Beethoven to Bartók, from Botticelli to Picasso. On the other hand, although it is only their equations that are infallible, the scientists themselves today are enjoying an aura of infallibility. To a certain extent we expect of them that they will solve all our problems. And for that reason society reveres and protects the scientist as it might its creator! In truth, the pursuit of science divorced from art, as much, at least, as art divorced from science, leads to an atrophying of all sense of human and communal responsibility, and the shirking of one's obligations to one's fellow-men.

THIRD THEME: EDUCATION

The fact that today anyone can learn of the exchange of matter and energy in textbooks does not make of that person an Einstein, and too often we believe that education consists in the cramming of facts. This is not a fault in England alone; it is, rather, I think more peculiar to the United States and Russia; but above all it is a weakness of our own era. Again, facts are an end-product, which like end-products in food and applied science are in themselves not capable of further elaboration. Has anyone noticed how in conversation so often a bald assertion, naked and final, whether true or not, kills civilized talk? The child fed on nothing but end-products will be as stunted mentally as he is physically. I was appalled to read the other day of the proportion of retarded children in one of the richest suburbs of New York. I am sure that Naples or Mexico City cannot compete in this respect!

Recent trends suggest that it may be possible to evolve a system of education that would consist not of supplying the end-fact but rather in encouraging the process of thinking by with-holding the end-fact and only supplying the clues, much as when we read a detective novel; thus a child would not be told the earth is round; but it would be encouraged to postulate a shape that would fit in with observed phenomena. Of course this would be a much slower way of acquiring knowledge, but it would be more organic and more satisfactory, and the child would, in fact, pass through the various stages of humanity in the evolution of knowledge; much as in the prenatal stage the human foetus passed through previous transitional phases of evolution. The child might very well imagine a Hercules supporting the earth, and a God pushing the sun round; and it would gradually come to understand from within the compelling, primeval urge to comprehend, explain and correlate.

Third interlude. We try to make rules to control the unpredictable. This is only possible up to a point, as the unpredictable cannot be excluded and will take its toll. For instance, I wager that any person given the most regular and assured salary, working hours, pleasant life, commuting at regular times, and enjoying all the comforts of hot and cold water, with all the unpredictable elements completely eliminated, will either commit suicide or rush to the gambling casino, where the unpredictable awaits him in its lowest form; or in a group, smaller or larger, he will set out to kill—for what is killing but the supreme game of chance? And is it not evident, in books and films, how the greatest attraction to the largest public is found in mystery, horror and unpredictability? Again, neither our private nor our collective existence has a sufficiently broad basis in thinking and feeling and wanting, nor does our society always succeed in integrating the narrow, smaller and more intense elements into a harmonious whole.

FOURTH THEME: LIBERTY AND OBEDIENCE

Checks and balances (or the antagonism of opposites together with a built-in system of counterweights) are inherent in nature. There is not a single thing in the universe which if unchecked, uncountered, would not, of itself, impose its own likeness on the whole of creation. (Of course—to our good fortune!—there is no such thing as a single thing, for even the tiniest thing in the world is already two things—a duality of interlocked, opposing, and balancing forces.) This is because, as we have stressed, each grain of matter is vested with eternity and infinity (time-space), and would wish, in its material embodiment, to express this urge in action and in the domination of all matter.

In that way, the intuitive, which corresponds to the artistic, is as much part of the will to infinity—in its crudest forms, for instance in the will of dust, as in the Sahara, to extend its domain, or of a particular religion to convert multitudes, in the will of germs to invade all living tissue, in the will of mice to populate the world, in the will of a Hitler to place himself and that figment of his phantasy the Aryan race atop the world—as it is sublimated in the will of a Van Gogh, or a Bach or a Bartók, to reach the very limits of our infinite depth and to express the inexpressible.

In this context, what is liberty? Pure liberty, or the complete abandonment of restraints, is a veritable impossibility except in the creative act, sublimated through discipline, purification and form in art. Pure liberty could only exist theoretically for one single smallest grain of matter alone, for it would imply the subjugation of everything else. As we know that this is impossible, as nature, the universe in its very foundation demonstrates the duality of all phenomena, we must admit that, as soon as two things co-exist, pure liberty is divided by half.

It stands to reason, therefore, that human liberty in the aggregate can only approach perfection and a measure of balanced probability to the degree that each conscious person can be imbued with the principles of equal rights for all his fellow-men, all his fellow-tenants in nature—and conversely he must realize his own composite nature, which, if not organized, self-disciplined, and brought within a harmonious unifying purpose, would disintegrate.

The choice before mankind is between (1) obedience to an outside authority, and (2) obedience to a self-imposed, inner authority—the highest form of which is exemplified in the lives of great saints, the holy men of India, or as sometimes expressed by artists in a masterpiece or simply in a spontaneous perfect action. Between the two extremes there are infinite shadings and gradations. These depend on the degree to which authority is broadly based and on the degree to which obedience is voluntary, as well as to the degree to which it is exercised for the common good, not only of the governed of a particular country but also of mankind as a whole.

At the one extreme is the tyrant wreaking his personal vengeance on the submissive multitude; at the other the holy man, who is beyond all external coercion. We choose our gods accordingly. Blind and uncritical obedience involves a deadening of the spirit and body and imposes the acceptance of continual discomfort—with its imposition of a will other than our own. This is a dangerous situation for man, inasmuch as it is not the sudden fatal onslaught of accident or disease that alone might ruin the species, but far more insiduously, the persistent, day-by-day erosion, the growing of the protective callous, which we accept docilely, deadening our instincts and our intuition, and which in the end account for the most hopeless diseases, spiritual and physical alike, of mankind.

When we cease to feel for others, and for ourselves, when we cease to know what constitutes the utterly care-free, the completely right, the healthy, the just, and only therefore, at long last, the prolongably spontaneous, we must be utterly miserable. It is then that our nature seeks refuge in the pathological wishful dreams of madmen.

Fourth interlude. May I propose another pair of axioms:

No. 1. *Our dreams and wishes are much more likely to come true to the degree that they are not for ourselves in the narrowest sense, and that we do not attempt to bring them about wilfully and ruthlessly.* All the virtues of perseverance, dedication, faith and humility are always essential to any object, but we must not and dare not ask or demand anything for ourselves, nor can we know exactly when or where our wish may be fulfilled, though one bright day, like a miracle, it will be. Wishes achieved in any other way can only be narrow, restricted victories, and are bound to collapse in the collapse of the greater unit—family, group, nation, etc.—though each of these units must maintain, within measure, its own integrity and autonomy.

No. 2. *Conversely, all our fears are inevitably realized to the degree that they are for ourselves exclusively.* Selfish fear paralyses mind and body, and we await our executioner as helpless passive victims.

FIFTH THEME: SOCIETY

My last example is the field of society and its ordering—what I call the relative within and without.

Let us imagine a large cross, of which the two intersecting beams are infinite in their length. The horizontal one would represent from left to right (or vice versa if we write Hebrew) past, present and future, and the vertical one mankind itself, and nature. Reading this time from the bottom upwards we would recognize the various qualities and quantities, in degree and kind, of an awareness of and interaction with our environment. Each of these qualities exists in the automatic as well as in the conscious —in the raw as in the sublimated. For man is part animal, either carnivorous (hunting, pillaging and destructive of accumulated wealth, often a purgative function) or herbivorous and cultivating (producing wealth)—and part whatever he wants to be. Even at his rawest, he justifies his primitive behaviour to his conscious mind by sublimating it.

These qualities are perhaps four, and we are all a combination of these in various proportions. 1. The muscular or physical, dominating in the material; 2. the visceral, or sensual, or acquisitive; 3. the nervous, co-ordinating or intellectual; and 4. the spiritual, which is aesthetic and moral and embraces that which lies beyond our immediate selves and to which we ultimately belong.

I would like to submit that a good society must accord to each a place and a share in its life. Let us begin with the physical. It ruled the cavemen, and still takes its toll today as it did in Nazi Germany. Of all peoples the Germans had developed in the highest form the capacity for abstract thought, so abstract and so principled that in fact it finally lost all contact with the human. The excesses in the physical and visceral field are a direct result of this imbalance.

If mankind's basic physical nature is not respected, either in man-to-man combat as in sport, or in struggles of man against nature as in mountain climbing, or man against himself as in violin-playing, or in philosophy, this nature will assert itself in anti-social behaviour.

And at the top of our vertical beam we have the spirit—a sense of all of which we are a serving part, a sense of the mystery and the for ever unknown which surrounds us, a sense of ultimate order and purpose which we may only apprehend, but which bespeaks a greater power. As we know, there exists no smallest grain of matter which does not partake of infinity and eternity. Such instinct and philosophy were once the realm of religions— so often pure in their conception and abused in application. I would like in this connection to propose a subject for urgent discussion—it is: 'How soon can a basic metaphysic and theology be incorporated in our school curriculum, evolved upon and with the collaboration of existing religions, but none the less independent of these?' What form would it take? I believe a form along the lines we have been contemplating. It would have to be a system in which all opposites were reconciled; in which art and science and religion would inspire each other; in which principles of change and evolution together with those of our crystallized, eternal certainties, of stillness with action, would find a place. The grandest and the smallest, the most generous and the meanest would have to be understood and related to each other within one great canvas.

As we are flesh and blood our symbols must be these same sublimated. Our symbols must include, according to the nature and inclination of each person, a philosophy, or a saint's life (Christ's, the Buddha's), a book, a painting, a string quartet, a church; or even in a different way, a flower, a tree, a butterfly— anything in fact which can confer or communicate a sense of the ideal and of a greater order to which we belong beyond our immediate selves. A society which does not include fasting and prayer, and of which at least a few members are not inclined to these forms of purification and identification with the infinite, is gravely unbalanced.

Our horizontal beam representing past, present and future is equally an integral part of the structure or pattern, and no society can be balanced unless it lives and thinks in these terms, unless in other words the past and the future each have a living voice in its people, its customs, and its administration.

In pre-Red China the past exercised a strangle-hold on the population to the exclusion of present and future. Today we see the inescapable violent reaction in a nation sacrificing all for the future: again a state of imbalance. As the 'present' in China was at all times too poor to possess any vested interests or to exercise any conservative restraint, the swing was complete and extreme.

In England the balance between past and future is perfect, and this nation has produced a race of statesmen able to think historically as no other nation. As with a great tree, or a happy marriage, certain results, the most precious and the rarest in terms of quality and depth, and those which cannot be acquired in any other way, can only come about as a result of the measured passage of time. This lends an increasing value to the investment of the ages, far exceeding the purely material gains of stocks or bonds.

If I may say so, the present is beginning to exercise too great an influence. At the centre of our beams, where they bisect each other, is man. He is at his smallest and narrowest in pain. The world and the universe diminish cruelly with stomach-ache and sea-sickness! He is again at his smallest and narrowest when he excludes past and future from his working-day dimensions and feels that these (the past and the future) owe him more than he owes them. We seem to be mortgaging both. If mankind or any society in particular persists in this mentality, they are in for a rude and bitter awakening.

The people of the United States, who are blessed with such great opportunities for achievement and success, and at the lowest level plagued with mere change (as in fashions) within the span of a single lifetime or less, are inclined to focus too strongly on the present at the expense of past and future.

Thus we can see that danger is ever-present. In pain or discomfort our vision narrows, as again in comfort and assurance we may become arrogant and in a different way irresponsible.

Self-sacrifice to the greater as well as to the future will always remain the noblest of human aspirations. The raising of our young (I refer to *homo-sapiens*), the cultivation, protection and love of things not only shorter-lived than ourselves, the planting of trees, the achievements of balance in society and the responsibility of guiding and helping the weaker and less evolved, while learning from them those secrets and qualities which they themselves have wrested from living nature—these are duties, missions and tasks, the performance of which is a measure of the maturity of a society. England again stands high in this respect.

I should like to add a word about the 'relative within and without'. The first degree of within is the womb and the stomach, the one to create, and the other to break down material into its component factors. These are, of all processes, matters of immediacy, of the most urgent present moment. With these our universe exists only in the now and here. In mankind's history these processes have always been associated with pain, although it need not always be so. Then in expanding degrees of time and size we have the whole body or the person, the family, the group, the region, the city, country, world and universe. Each one of these relative degrees is both within and without a smaller one or a greater one. A balance must be preserved between each, as we are each one of us a composite of all. Sometimes we must return to restrict ourselves, or take refuge in the first degree; sometimes we soar to the highest; indeed sometimes the two extremes are very closely intertwined. Too many of us seek a shelter within the compact mass of society, and within a particular country, and within the world, in the sense that we do not objectively see the dangers facing us. It is incredible to think that on the eve of any great war the cinemas are full, the people are buying, they are building houses, they are in other words numbed to the without. Within reason this is a healthy protective device; exaggerated, it is suicide.

We need a more perfect balance between the objective and the subjective, the aristocratic and the democratic. Again in England the balance is more easily preserved, in that it is an island, and one is therefore so easily 'without' (beyond) the confines of civilization and security. The high seas intrude to within yards of the cosiest cottage.

There must at all times be people who have the trust of society sufficiently to be able to explore this 'outside', and to appear as outsiders, while society full well knows that they belong and can be trusted. In a continental mass, as the United States or Russia, this is sometimes more difficult, because of the sheer distance to the outside, and then again, because of the movement of population within the great multitude that have not allowed it to develop sufficiently the stability, the security and the trust between its elements which would enable some of them to appear independent, or eccentric, or able to view their own difficulties with objectivity.

Today in a tangible way the stars are very much part of our 'without', and almost our 'within'. As a species we require this dual, counterbalancing orientation. In the past the 'without' was represented to our physical selves exclusively as the neighbour's dwelling or land. Today it is a distant star. If anything can possibly bring about world co-operation towards greater ends it is that henceforth man's threshold is not only his home and family, or race or country, but the new dimension, the planetary one of world, as opposed and related to other worlds. This, the expanding universe and search for knowledge, bringing with it dire penalties for all of mankind, must, we hope, keep us all in leash and on our best behaviour. It is as if mankind as a whole were thrown into a life-boat on a rough sea. People who have hated each other, together with those who have loved, each of whom is functional to the survival of that life-boat, are thrown together. The danger is, of course, that each one alone might wreck it! Only one of the lot, hating a little too much or about to die, with no stake in the future, could out of impatience, mistaken heroics or spite, bore a hole in the boat and thus sink the whole company.

Is it not evident that mankind, in its constant and unremitting search for cheap solutions and its trust in its false gods, mainly in its wrong habits of thinking, seems to be positively flocking to the labour camps and to suicide of every description, from cancer to atomic explosions, and from the penitentiary to the asylum? And that is largely so because the artistic and the creative way of life has been sacrificed. The inspired thought is often shunned and disgraced unless it bear the official stamp of approval. A few people are caged and well fed to play various concertos and to dance, and to this end contests are held. Others are well fed and trained as are police dogs. But let us thank God that despite all the human spirit is unpredictable: it cannot remain trapped for ever in hermetically sealed canisters. The heretic human spirit is not a specialized affair, it is not a trick, it is not a technique, it is part of the ignition system of the universe. It is the divine spark that inhabits every grain of matter in the universe. It cannot be trapped or enslaved by ruler, system, doctrine, or narrow specialization, but when stamped out in one form will, we trust, emerge in another. Let us keep open the connections whereby this human spirit may freely move between the arts and the sciences and thus make more of each. May we thus become better violinists, scientists, artists, writers, and above all, better human beings, by enlarging and enriching our personal needs to include each other's.   LONDON, 1959

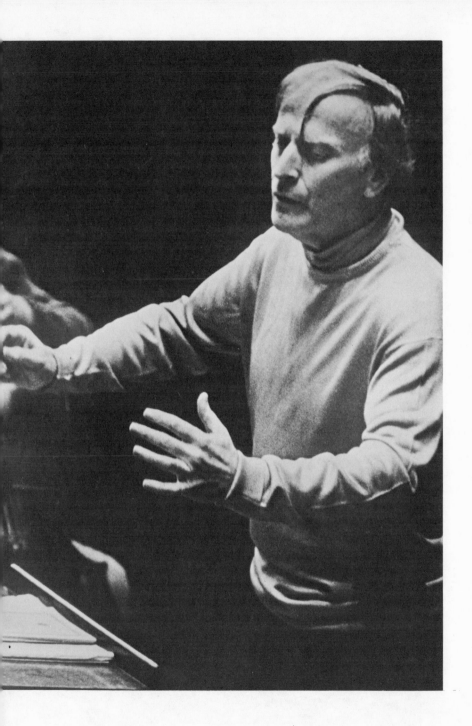

Above: with Diana and sons Gerard and Jeremy

Below: with sisters Hephzibah and Yaltah

Part Three: The Environment

17. Heaven on Earth

MAN TODAY has created as vicious and vindictive a God as ever extorted the tribute of a superstitious people. The dragon we worship enshrines the inanimate and consumes the animate: only the clank of metal survives the devastation of species, and for all the human courage and sacrifice spent, only the coins and the weapons dug up centuries from now may bear testimony to the madness of the once-living.

But need it be so? Can we not subjugate the inanimate and enshrine the living? Life on earth exists on a severely limited budget. With each generation mankind has multiplied, but only in recorded times has he ceased enlarging his capital, life's organic capital, and only very recently has he been approaching at accelerating pace the limits of this budget. Oxygen, sweet water, green leaves and topsoil—these are but a few of the essential elements of life which have become exhaustible.

Privately most of us know the limits of our personal financial budgets, and when we exceed these only the culprit and his dependants suffer. Humanity, however, just like many an individual, has not yet learned that its survival depends upon resources that until now have been mostly free and apparently infinite. Money and weapons are merely measures of *relative* wealth and power *between* groups of human beings: they can never form the basis for the absolute balance-sheet which is that of all life, man included, with nature. God, the banker, does not deal in gold. His equity is life's respect for life, humanity's collective investment in the living and in the organic.

Our weapons and so many of our tools have been reduced to weapons against nature, if not against man. However necessary they may be for relative survival, they are ultimately an investment in the dead. Our exploitation of man, woman and child, our extermination of species, as of recognizably different fellow-men, is an investment in death. Money and weapons cause instant effect, but can either grow a tree?

Our greatest efforts seem to serve to increase our dependence on that fire-breathing dragon with metal scales and a fissionable heart. As our dependence increases, so does the volume of our propitiatory sacrifices: we have discovered how to sacrifice not only present generations, but future ones as well. Now at least, and at last, we know this cannot go on for ever: it cannot even go on another fifty years.

Heaven will come to mankind when we learn to respect our limits. It may sound paradoxical to say that the infinity and eternity of Heaven is in reality only the distance to the heart of a stranger, to the heart of an enemy: eternity is the instant of recognition. To recognize truth is to win the trust of the innocent and the weaker.

God told man he was to be custodian of all life. Other animals, all kinds everywhere, were there for his pleasure: but pleasure involves protection. Is this not the case with our wives, our husbands, our children, our dogs, our trees? Is not our pleasure synonymous with their well-being, their security, independence and satisfaction? Why indeed is the concept 'for our pleasure' taken to mean 'at our mercy?' And if these objects that are essential to our pleasure, and indeed to our survival, are now largely at our mercy, must this not imply the injunction of mercy and protection to all things at our mercy? As Shakespeare with his infinite sensitivity said: 'The quality of mercy is not strained, it droppeth as the gentle rain from heaven upon the place beneath . . .'

Our pleasure, everyone's pleasure, must be found henceforth in the non-competitive and the non-exploitative.

In recent millenia the human race has thrown up quite a few men who have seen the emerging truth of man's condition and have exhorted us to 'Turn the other cheek,' or 'Do unto others . . .'. The supreme example was Gandhi's precept of non-violence. Now we have reached the stage in man's evolution when we can no longer afford to crucify, poison or shoot our wisest men, or even belatedly to canonize them: we are now at the very gates of Heaven or, if we choose, of Hell.

What is this Heaven on Earth? The stress should be first on

individuals and secondarily on interests, because the former are
the heart and bloodstream of the latter. Here are a few rough
definitions.

1. Our technology would live within our budget. At no time
   would it be allowed to deplete capital resources and resources essential to future generations of all life: nor would
   our technology be allowed to produce waste or poisonous
   matter not absorbable into the stream of life, or prejudicial
   to the quality of life.
2. Our technology would be made infinitely more refined and
   flexible. Power from the sun, tides, earth-core, differences
   of temperature would be delivered unobtrusively, discreetly,
   noiselessly to the user. It would be a technology encouraging
   to regional and individual diversity by its infinite flexibility.
3. Organizational, administrative and bureaucratic structures
   would offer a maximum of approaches and cross influences
   between governed and governor, the greatest possible
   adaptability to individual needs. Schools would be geared to
   every character and interest and requirement.
4. Education would inculcate a contemporary morality drawn
   from and built upon all religions, but relevant to our era,
   its discoveries, its responsibilities, its maturity, its revelations.
5. It would be admitted humbly and wisely that everything is
   not for everybody, nor can humanity any longer do everything in its power. There would be diversity of ambitions
   and a newly interpreted feudal structure (by feudal I mean
   not service given vertically to the baron above one, but the
   fee that each and every human being should pay laterally to
   his fellow-man as part of his debt to life itself, which might
   cure the crippling narcissism that commercialism and its
   Mephisto advertising has evoked in us all); a structure in
   which money or power alone would no longer remain the
   chief yardstick of achievement, but a pride and a humility of
   function and a respect for another's function, be he land-
   owner or garbageman (actually the garbageman should
   represent the first stage to resurrection, for he is the
   retriever!), a working faith and a trust in the slow and
   inevitable distillation of excellence, in the course of a lifetime, in the course of generations, provided it is achieved in

ceaseless confrontation and through constant reassessment between ourselves, our fellow-men and our environment. A new appreciation would be sought, a new cultivation of our senses and of our intuition, a respect and an honesty in dealing with life, beauty and truth.

I have used the word 'feudal' deliberately to evoke a concept which still carries, and quite rightly, many reprehensible connotations: the wretched condition of serfs from Russia to Ireland, the exploitation not so much of conditions of the land as of the peasant—these were the abuses which condemn feudalism. But what about words like 'capitalism' in China, 'communism' in Texas, or 'Christianity' in certain areas of the Middle East? Yet each one of these has contributed a very valuable ingredient or two to humanity's cumulative experience and wisdom. In like manner and in the same way I would wish an enlightened Moslem to speak about Christianity, an enlightened capitalist to analyse communism, and so on. The catch of course is that it would take a real Christian to do so, and all who are Christian in name only are from my point of view not really Christian. In the same way it is essential to break down blind and prejudiced reflexes against different ways of life, different concepts of existence from which we can always retrieve and distil a valuable lesson and learn a few pointers.

Progress is not inevitable nor continuous. Forgive me, therefore, if in line with my concept of the respect and curiosity due to every human manifestation from witchcraft to polytheism I offend with a word, but not with my heart.

From feudalism, from communism too, there is something to learn, something to conserve. The spirit of conservation must often, like the gold prospector, sift a mountain of pebbles and sand for one nugget of gold. There are quite a few manifestations of the human spirit that are totally bad, but even they must be carefully studied to yield not inspiration, but warning of the way in which the partly bad or rotten can become wholly bad and rotten. Nazi Germany was one such example.

To return to our perception of our environment: must we for ever assault our senses or condemn them to their lowest uses? There is no need for mankind to remain imprisoned within his mechanism of aggression and defence. The eye is better when trained to observe through painting, architecture, sculpture, drawing, or through the eyepiece of a telescope or microscope, than it is in sighting through a rifle; the ear through music and lovely sounds, and so on for all our five senses.

We have so much to live for beyond mere attack and defence: these we gradually evolve through the generations and within each lifetime, and finally transform into their opposite expression —the creative act, as of a painter, sculptor, composer, architect, or the creative vision of an inspired scientist.

As a musician, I am accustomed to the sublimation and transfiguration of emotions, thoughts, motives and acts. Surely if the artist indulged in the reverse process of reverting to primal motives, he might be the criminal of all time—but one easily caught, for by my very definition he would act out of his first impulse. And we would have no art. For it is the very removal from and distance between primitive desires and sublimated realization which spells the quality of human expression. Literature that is merely a photographic record of acts can never be great literature, and certainly never be poetry. Knowledge and beauty do not require quantitative material corroboration. Truth is true even if proved only once; moreover it will never be within the bounds of possibility for every man to tread the surface of the moon: he must be content to dream and write about it and express it in his art.

One of the most disturbing symptoms of the superstitition of our day I referred to at the beginning, that blind faith in a monstrous god so antagonistic to man and his art, is our passion for the abstraction. Our obsession with and prostration in front of the scientific abstract induces a mania for reducing the name to the cipher. We can see this in the complete and unnecessary removal of such convenient memory aids to London telephone numbers as Whitehall or Archway, which are in fact a shorthand for three numbers and a reminder of human origin.

A genuine innovation for the better is still highly suspect, but a change authorized by the venal high priests of our age is embraced with meek dutifulness and trust.

To call a child, we shall soon be saying 'Hey, 427,' just as with our car licence-plates. At least with our licences the practicability of combined alphabet and numerals has been recognized!

We will no longer say 'My mother', 'my child', 'my Queen', but will cite a cipher which only the computer will react to. Perhaps 'My God!', will be something like 'No. 1, Latitude 60, Longitude 65'. That way lies madness and destruction.

One great characteristic of life is its aspiration towards uniqueness. As we rise in the consciousness of life, this hallmark becomes ever more pronounced. Although no doubt every crystal snowflake is recognizably unique, and so must every leaf be different, only man can so savagely distort the concept of uniqueness as to equate it with the idea of being himself only—above and at the expense of all others. Uniqueness, which should be a doctrine of mutually respected variety, can become in man the doctrine of tyranny.

Man must pursue his knowledge and understanding of nature and of himself not with the object of domination and the extension of power, but in a way in which awe and humility before the mystery of life and nature grow in equal proportion to his knowledge.

Man must retain his veneration for nature. That short period of simple-minded and vainglorious confidence in man's capacity to reconstruct nature is finally giving way to a conception of the magnitude to which we belong and the complexity which we are.

Only in the last weeks it has been revealed that the genetic code in a microscopic bacterium allows for 20 million variables or possibilities for each single individual: in a human being these possibilities are of the order of 12 billion. To calculate the weather, the micro-climate of an area only 15 miles square, the factors and variables are so complex that to cope with them would necessitate a computer extending from London to Moscow. Such is the order of variety in the environment.

Our main concern is to allow this almost infinite range of free, automatic choice—genetic and otherwise—to remain undamaged, and to guide the choice towards ideals of beauty and perfection. So far our deliberate efforts towards change have for the most part only reduced and damaged our potentialities, as for instance through radiation, and debased our ideals and multiplied our monsters. This is true not only figuratively, but literally, for they are born in greater numbers than ever before.

I have always wished that in our age of comparative studies, in addition to anthropology—which was one of the first, thanks to Darwin—and along with comparative religions, that comparative political systems would be assessed for their qualities, defects, timeliness and achievements. For my part I can conceive of many permutations and commutations, but to my mind the lucky societies will always be those which are blessed with a hereditary, constitutional monarchy as Head of State. For constitutional monarchy is one of the most evolved, beneficent, organic and civilizing manifestations of the human spirit, the distillation through generations of the crude tyrant into the living human symbol of unity in diversity, of tolerance and respect.

In past ages, before man discovered the common denominators of science, in biology and finally in psychology, he viewed each phenomenon as separate, assigning deities to each. With one God, however, he began to see relationships, and to discover the broad lines of a basic structure. He also began to gather together his fellow-men—into armies, into bands of slaves, or for that matter into groups of Christians.

We are beginning to emerge from this crudeness and this brutal conception of 'order' as we discover an infinity of differentiating degrees between contrasting phenomena, degrees which link opposites as in an arc link.

Now, having achieved this, we must begin finally to cultivate, to respect, to delight in variety. We must formulate the philosophy and the morality which sees every act of blind and automatic multiplication as a gesture of death, whether it be the endless piling up of apartment blocks or the repetitive motions of a factory worker.

By and large man now—to achieve his Heaven—must nurture, cherish, revel in every variety of life, every manifestation of colour, language, dress, gesture he can see, hear or study. Man's great destiny is to bring the infinite variety of life into harmony, but decidedly not to reduce it to uniformity and false order.

Perhaps the most misused words at the moment are 'progress' and 'order'; one must ask 'progress where?' and 'whose order?'. These words still carry a romantic echo, just as democracy, socialism and the much-regretted concept of freedom (freedom for what?) did until recently.

I would suggest a new crusade, a new slogan—one already

discernible among the younger generation, though perhaps not yet spelled out in its full implication. '*Create and conserve beauty. Destroy ugliness and replace it with beauty*.' Is it not fortunate that by divine coincidence what we most desperately need is also beautiful? Sewage is neither beautiful nor healthful (albeit useful indirectly); oxygen is purest where green plants and open space are at hand; pure water flows in bubbling streams where salmon thrive.

Imagine the opposite! Imagine that oxygen were only available in cylinders at the bottom of coal-pits and that we had to drink sewage for health! That this nightmarish myth has all but become a reality in some urban industrial areas is an uncomfortable thought.

By ugliness I mean not only the obvious assaults upon our senses—visual, aural, our sense of smell, of taste; not only offences against our innate, instinctive and intellectual sense of balance, proportion and reason, but equally the ugliness of human facial expressions conditioned by preoccupation with suppression, aggression, fear, hypocrisy, false values, moral superiority, cruelty, exploitation, greed; so much of sickness and disease is a result either immediate or once-removed of these causes. We all know too about the horrors of thalidomide and cyclamates, and no doubt a thousand other death-dealing substances to come.

By beauty I mean the constant search and effort to create in all objects which we use and handle, in all activities, and foremost in ourselves, expressions of nobility and exaltation, as of humour and compassion, each as different, varied, personal and particular as possible. This cannot happen suddenly. Money, a freely exchangeable currency, will always be needed; it is in fact in many ways one of the blessings of civilization; but as we cannot buy everything we covet, so too, by the same token, we cannot convert all things into money. Wars will still happen, engulfing millions of people in agony; plagues and famine too; but above all this must be borne high the greatest obligation, the most binding duty of mankind: to redeem one's fellow-man from ugliness.

I believe that most people in Britain and the Western countries are becoming aware of these issues. There have been many recent articles on conservation, for instance. For my part, by conservation I do not mean the conservation of everything intact—

as of a corpse. I mean the conservation of everything beneficial and life-maintaining bequeathed by nature to man, and the conservation of every expression of man's need for beauty. The Georgian squares of London are one example; the blue whale another; the few remaining oak forests a third, to name but a few at random.

I also mean the conservation of things, values and institutions which represent a very long, expensive and painful investment of experience. Today with our instant, explosive, and brutal shock-methods we threaten all and everything which has taken time, centuries and millenia to accumulate, to achieve. So long as man belongs to the animal kingdom, so long as he is born of flesh and blood, so long as man and woman join in the creative act—so long is he bound to the realm of nature.

Regardless of how far his intellect may explore the world of inorganic matter, for his pleasures, his pains, his fulfilment and peace of mind, he belongs to the pulsating life he shares with his frail and fragile co-breathers on this earth.

As with 'progress' and 'order', so too there is ambiguity in the different interpretations of the word 'conservation'.

Our ear, so dominated by man-made change, and by the new, has lent the word 'conservation' a rather dusty connotation. It has lost the commanding concern of maintaining, of conserving a way of life—our way of life, and implies a somewhat charitable, almost superfluous concern with a fossilized preservation in suspended states of alien matter.

It is hard to drive home that total concept of life on earth, of ecological unity, which makes us all at least as dependent upon all life as we are competitive with all life.

When I speak of conservation, I have in mind the defence of humanity, of the living protoplasm which has struggled with and triumphed over the vast mass of inorganic, molten, cooling matter. I speak of defending our global heritage, this life-promoting environment which is our only defence against the timeless inanimate—the ageless dragon whom we worship, now clothed in steel, plutonium and plastic, which has risen to new powers to challenge all life anew, even as we assume we are about to dominate it.

Naturally, at the lowest level life is overwhelmingly competitive, but this is because each species fills only one segment of the ecological structure of life; it is one thread in the pattern of a gigantic, interwoven, living and changing tapestry, of which it is not aware. Here stability and continuity are achieved by the automatic checks and balances of opposing forces, by their own, individual, inbuilt limitations and restrictions, and by the fact that all destruction of life, i.e. death from all causes, only enriches and builds up the reserves of living matter. Thus even our fuel is provided by coal, the material remains of plant life, and oil, the material remains of animal life.

Man, however, has raised himself by grafting himself on to bigger and bigger brains (now about to be done surgically) to a position from where he can see a goodly part of that living tapestry, even while his native physical equipment has fallen away: claws, fangs, fur, armour, even wings he has forsworn biologically, though in league with the inanimate demon, he has manufactured all of these, with a vengeance! But the cruder defensive and aggressive means belong by right only to the fractionally alive, because as we reach the higher levels of life and as we enjoy a broader view of our living tapestry, the competitive requirements of survival must give way to the collaborative requirements of both survival and society.

When we begin to identify ourselves not only with the immediate in time and place—as does, say the ant—but with life generally everywhere, we must, logically, depend for our survival upon the broad realm that we perceive, upon which we exercise effect, and for which we are therefore responsible.

As a musician I live with vibrations, phenomena which are neither animate nor inanimate, but common to both states. Vibrations are of all phenomena the ones which allow us to touch, as it were, the most distant source, both in space and time. Because we are vibrating, pulsating beings, we can sense and in fact relive the sensations, sentiments, impulses and thoughts of thousands of other musicians, and as musicians we can communicate these to millions of people.

When I speak of conservation as a musician, it is not only in terms of wonderful illuminated manuscripts from the Middle Ages, but in terms of their actual sound, the complex of vibrations they set in motion in the human mind.

My Heaven on Earth is not a museum, nor a static state of unlikely bliss, but a situation fraught with problems and challenges, ones that would absorb tremendous amounts of courage, curiosity, effort, patience, dedication and self-sacrifice. But above all, my Earth-Heaven is for me the acceptance by civilized man of those bonds which make all life interdependent and which make of us conscious custodians of the future.

After all, we already determine our future; we condemn it in fact when we say 'après moi le déluge.' I am afraid that death, pain and disappointment are an intrinsic part of my Heaven, but suffering would, I hope, not be inflicted deliberately by selfish men, blind and deaf to the consequences of their actions.

Perhaps the greatest importance must be attached to the inculcation of a respect for continuity, a respect for all life, a sense of relative values, and a readiness to admit error. By relative values I mean, for instance, the multiplication of cars and roads without building a commensurate organization for handling road accidents. I mean the production of jet and internal combustion engines and nuclear bombs without any thought of the amount of pollution our living atmosphere can absorb. I mean the infliction of untold horror in the name of liberty, democracy, communism and socialism. I mean the multiplication of both the sick and their care without the measures necessary for preventive medicine. I mean the exploitation of life for greed and power, as formerly in slavery and child labour, and as now at the other extreme of consumer power, in which the appetite is constantly irritated and whetted for the purpose of profit, so that the market can depend upon a continuously unsatisfied and restless people.

Each time we irreversibly destroy an organic element on our planet, we are cutting the ground from under our own feet; we are destroying our own living tissues and those of our children and our children's children. We are destroying the helpless water and air, the helpless leaves, the helpless blood cells and bone marrow of living flesh.

The problem that faces us now is actually behind us and beside us too, that is to say we have to think spherically, as it were, to see synoptically and to learn to live and judge at two levels: the visionary long-term one and the day-to-day one.

Immediates are indissolubly linked to ultimates, the wind to the whirlwind: sow the one and you will reap the other, and with the frightening acceleration of our present age neither King nor Head of State can hope for the 'deluge' to overtake his successor —the likelihood is that he will be drowned in the instant after-effects of his own actions.

Will this shrinking of time-space evoke greater caution in the wrong sense? More conservative reaction in the negative sense? Or will we be able to expand and extend our minds, become aware but not frightened of dangers, consider responsibilities the inevitable concomitant of rights, and find dignity in being an active part of a general community, instead of an isolated cog in a wheel that seems to turn to ever smaller and less worthy purposes?

Do we know what we should conserve? Can we agree upon it? I think of the good burgher of Bath who recently could only envisage a particularly beautiful sweep of lawn, not as had the eighteenth-century architect to whom it was an intrinsic part of the design of his terrace, but as 'a criminal waste of building space'. Must short-term finance always dictate to us? The disastrous results of such a policy have been shown in this last decade in America, where the structure of the cities of the nineteenth century mainly as huge market places has so alienated the human being that those who cannot escape to the suburbs stay behind to be mugged (or, if they are lucky, to mug others).

Must fear of other men, of ourselves, for ever determine our behaviour? If the human creature could advance in goodwill, tolerance and self-abnegation at the same speed as he has with his scientific inventions; if he could replace his lost faith in the institutional religions with a real sense of the stake each and every member of the human race has in the human condition, then we might see a fresh flowering of the spirit of man and a redressing of the sad imbalance visible to the young, who search for values and find none, who have weighed us, the older generation, in the balance and found us wanting.

Solomon said: 'A wise man's heart discerneth both time and judgement.' How far we still are from this wise man! And yet our only hope for self-preservation is just the exercise of this, the ability to focus on the far-off while dealing with the everyday.

1970

18. Architecture Today

ARCHITECTURE seems to me to have a certain quality of nostalgia, and the eye of the architect to be looking backward, for a building is fundamentally a man-made womb—and perhaps therein lies its chief inherent contradiction in terms and its basic fault. However, it must also embody man's adult aspirations, in terms not only of cubic feet of space and air, but also of harmony, security, excitement, peace, elegance, grandeur, nobility and strength, if not power, arrogance and ruthlessness.

Architecture, as much as a forest of trees, must grow out of the ground it stands on; it must *belong*, it must tell us about the particular people who dwell in it and use it—how they differ from other people; it must reveal the local peculiarities of soil, climate and topography.

Again, however important planning is for a city—particularly for the broad lines of flow, the style or styles, the public buildings, great vistas, main avenues, the separation of different kinds of traffic, the setting aside of interlocking parks and quiet green squares—planning must never override the instinctive and spontaneous growth of a city in accordance with its population's pace, habits and requirements.

For instance, who could plan the design of a fingerprint, which for that very reason is recognizable individually? Yet the medieval towns of Italy and Germany, the Trulli villages of south-east Italy, old Paris with its streets of every width and at every angle, its sudden changes of perspective as one rounds a corner, are living sources of joy and surprise, of stimulation and satisfaction, which never pale.

At all times we must have glimpses of sky and trees, and at no time should we tolerate either the narrow canyons between skyscrapers or the maddening long horizontal lines of enormous buildings or sequences of buildings, which actually because they are straight become twisted in perspective, and twist the mind and the heart both of the onlooker and the dweller. The ancient Greeks already knew that you could not build a square-like or rectangle-like building as an uncompromising cube. Have we degenerated so far because our only criterion for human need is financial profit?

Socially too the new architecture is mainly lamentable, for not only does it trap and encapsulate individuals without giving them security—it makes a reality of all dreams of escape and violence. The large housing project often has no social amenities: churches, kindergartens, libraries, sculptors' studios, painters' studios, musicians' practice, rehearsal and performance rooms, clubs and pubs for the adult, Finnish baths, swimming baths, provision for sports of different kinds, these are all lacking from apartment blocks. There might also be rooms for the exhibition and interchange of residents' art, for the pursuit of cottage industries from shoe-making to knitting and pottery, with workshops, firing ovens, book and record libraries; also simple non-denominational and interdenominational cells, shrines and chapels (always provided with flowers and decorative offerings) for meditation and prayer. Outside there would be garden allotments for residents. But no: cages upon cages are built, with as little regard for humanity as for battery hens.

I for one move that piped music be severely excluded from all buildings as the affront it is to our senses and our keenness of perception. This mankind does not need, nor does any but a warped mentality want. What we *do* need is breathable air and potable water, both of which are becoming dangerously scarce.

Acoustics in our public rooms are abominable for the most part. In the foyer of the Queen Elizabeth Hall one can hardly hear oneself speak: the chatter and din of voices is unbearable. The same goes for the lighting, which is not only most unflattering to ladies but even to men—and this argument should carry some weight nowadays. Have many architects realized the importance of the placing of buildings in relation to the points of the compass? Each room and group of rooms should be planned for a proportion of sunlight and shade, of wind and shelter and peace.

Have many architects achieved the consummate skill with which simple mountain peasants have always placed their chalets? Personally, I am completely opposed to airtight buildings, particularly in relatively temperate climates above ground. Such buildings completely divorce the dweller from his environment, humanly and socially. There is no greater social cleavage in tropical countries than that between the air-conditioned classes and their exposed inferiors. England's wholesomeness, strength and democracy have sprung as much from the cracks and draughts in her buildings, I suggest, as from anything else. In the tropics I would rather build in sensible, suitable materials, using whitewashed adobe walls, with small and few windows, in the shade of trees, and as the wonderful Mohammedan civilization did, with running water inside and outside, soothing to the ear, cooling and delightful. Roofs could also be planted as gardens.

Leaving urban plans aside, I want to put in a word for the small dwelling in the country or the suburbs. People should again be able to build their own houses with their own hands, as the civilized Greek islanders do, or the Philippinos their houses on stilts, or as countless self-respecting civilizations have done in time past. Today the professional services of constructor and labourer are both too expensive and too crude, lacking as they mostly are in all real craftsmanship.

Building kits of adobe, wood, brick, lath, metal, according to local requirements and taste, should be available cheaply and practically to enable a family to build their own dwelling, and change it, enlarge it or diminish it as they may wish—to integrate it into their lives or their work.

Schools should teach child and adult an appreciation and understanding of building styles of all places and periods and their social function, in the way that attempts are now being made in the fields of painting and music. In fact, one of the most basic urges of the youngest children is to handle materials and build houses, as it is to make music. This instinct must be encouraged and given guidance through humanity's past experience, and not through a teacher's project only. Our eyes and ears, our senses of smell and taste and feel must be open and stimulated, not assailed and stuffed with any trash or makeshift which will fill the orifice.

And speaking of that, if we are to survive without becoming asphyxiated and suffocated with our own debris, the architect of towns and dwellings must take into account the cycle of matter, and should ensure the return of all organic matter to the soil, as is done in Edinburgh, for otherwise the city becomes a complete parasite upon its surroundings—a consuming cancer spreading contamination and waste and eventually destroying itself with its host, instead of providing a centre for the spirit and heart of man, for his intellect, his style and his culture.

LONDON, 1967

19. The Indian Contribution

AN ARTIST'S ECONOMY is very different from the economy behind the Gross National Product; in fact, it is akin to that of the Indian villagers. It is reckoned in the highest yield of human values—written, oral, religious, aesthetic and moral disciplines reflected as much in the smallest acts and gestures of daily life as in the greatest works of art—the highest yield in human values for the lowest consumption of goods. Rather the contrary principle, shall I say, to the economy regulating the commerce in spirits or drugs.

To the artist, as to the Indian villager, every flicker, every expression of life is precious. For him there is no wasted time, or wasted beauty. There is only the infinitely varied and eternal cycle of life, which embraces, for instance, the thousands of monkeys which used to inhabit the trees between Delhi and the airport only twenty years ago, and the cows, solemn and secure in their manifold contributions to village life.

One might say of the Indians that no other people today has achieved so high a civilization, so supreme in religious, artistic, scientific, literary, aesthetic, human and architectural accomplishments, all achieved with such joyous and reverent exuberance and with so little disruption of life or of the rootedness of life. What other people have known how to use their leisure so well? I remember many years ago when our beloved Homi Bhabha was first interviewed by *Time Magazine*, he was asked by a rather naïve young man how it was possible that so technologically retarded a country as India could produce a scientist, and other scientists, as advanced and formidable as Homi. Homi gave the classic and perfect answer. 'It is true,' he said, 'that India neither invented nor produced the motor-car, the refrigerator, the aeroplane, nor did it manufacture these in the overwhelming quantities of other industrialized countries, but for hundreds of years, during those

many months every year when the Indian peasant did not have
to work, he sat in the shade of a tree and thought.' And may I
add to Homi's words: the Indian peasant thought Truth, he did not
think enviously, grudgingly, hatefully, resentfully, or ambitiously
—he thought a philosophy of truth in life, and he thought as an
artist in action.

I would like to know if the commuter, fighting his way through
subway and motor traffic, if the tycoon pursuing his business deal
at the gambling casinos, if the children glued gaping to television
violence are enjoying their leisure, or merely mortgaging their
free time in further enslavement?

Tell me, which factory workers have improvised songs and
dances? The rural Indian, having washed his white dhoti
drying on the stones by a stream, understands full well that
the measure of a man's worth is not the power he wields, but is
rather a worth which survives and increases with his nakedness.
We often ask what a man is worth, with no thought of his mind
or brain, let alone his heart, his liver, or his spleen.

I am convinced the world is ripe for a new morality, which
is in fact the oldest of all. The most advanced Western type of
man, for instance, the astronaut, requires the virtues of a Yogi
guru: patience, self-control, finding comfort in one or two
asanas; able to survive isolation and loneliness, a restricted diet,
long meditations in silence, and requiring integrity and honesty.
These strapping American and Russian boys will soon be sent to
some ashram high up in the Himalayas, where perhaps China is
already training hers!

Speaking seriously, Indian *aptitudes*, which have proved what
child's play it is for this people to produce jet-planes, or even
H-bombs if, God forbid, required, must yield pride of place to
that peculiar Indian *wisdom* which need no longer be only con-
templative, retiring or passive, but must now, at our critical time,
seek universal application.

Whereas Indian beliefs have gone from the universal to the
particular, Western beliefs have been crawling from the particular
to the universal. Even today our religions do not concede
brotherhood to animal species, denying them soul, even as each
does to all different or non-believers, adherents of other religions
or sects. Only *this* attitude has permitted the institutionalized,

organized massacre of peoples and animals. It has taken the combined science of men like Galileo, Darwin, Newton and Einstein, together with a rediscovery of ancient Greek and Arab science, to outdistance the confining, constricting tenets, the dogmas of Western religions and political -isms, finally to establish the fact that the world *is* round. And in how many other ways is the earth *still* flat for most of us. In the light of this, we need not wonder at the overweening arrogance of science and technology in the West.

Indian conceptions of the divine, the universal and the eternal, together with Indian symbolic mythology, have never been at odds with truth, human, scientific or divine. I pray that in India science and knowledge may always remain where they belong— the *servants* of humanity, the *humble* explorers of divine mystery.

An important proportion of people in advanced technological societies are ill. Although we may understand and even justify a diseased condition, there is no excuse for condoning it, let alone encouraging it. In poorer countries, too, the same principle applies. Bilharzia, for instance, may be common to a large proportion of Egyptians, but this condition cannot be accepted for this reason as a human norm.

Unlike a large proportion of our Western population, the Indian peasant cannot afford suddenly to want what he has never known, he must simply put up with what he has—for never will the billion people of India and China own two cars per family or all die in a hospital. However, the cheapest of products—largely cancer-producing chemicals and bottled drinks —are reaching the multitudes, and only mass media—radio, television—are gaining their minds. But long before those extrapolated figures so dear to the heart of statisticians are achieved, oil pollution, radioactive wastes, and other bulk wastes, together with growing poverty and discomfort, and mental and physical disease, will have added their own swelling statistics into the general pot. The curve is not a simple one; for instance, rootlessness, a type of anonymous housing, colour television, processed foods and violence all interact together with a hundred more factors such as the lack of oral traditions and crafts.

The childish trust in the inevitable rise of living standards for *all* through industrialization must be exploded for the half-truth that it is. It is in large part a myth to perpetuate a still crude technology, which can only make an increasing part of the world impoverished and tributary, compelling it to depend on the satisfaction of appetites which can never be assuaged.

The right way around would be to reduce American, European and Japanese consumption, and in the meantime to explore and develop the great advances in knowledge and technology which will restore the ecological balance of life, the re-cycling and the salvation of so-called wastes, and which will lift the heavy and dead hand of the inorganic as it throttles our very life's blood.

India is in a remarkable position to achieve a real advance, a balanced two-pronged advance: human and technological. As the vast majority will never know the ownership of motor-engines and electrical house-aids until an advanced technology takes over, they cannot change their ways quickly enough to join the general suicidal gallop of the advanced countries. They must patiently wait to meet the better technology when it finally takes a form compatible with their human needs and their numbers. There is an urgent need for new techniques, and for new uncontaminating sources of power, no longer organic and fossil-powered, as coal or oil, nor inorganic, as atomic; no longer concentrated, that is, but permanent everywhere and diffuse: for instance, power from the sun and the heat of the inner earth as revealed in volcanoes. As an example, Holland and Switzerland, two of the most advanced countries in Europe, relied greatly upon the power of wind and water. The pollution and noise of jet air travel must give way to trains, propelled by linear electric power, floating through underground vacuum tunnels at speeds far beyond the speeds of sound. The surface of our planet must encourage life and beauty, not suicide.

Until such time as these advances are achieved, there must be great and unavoidable *restrictions* in the despoiling and sacking of humanity, of nature and of all life, past, present and future. Only thus will we be brought ever closer to the less criminal and guilty. One day we may become the humble pupil of the Indian villager.

India's vast population, which cannot even entertain the false dream of contemporary technological utopias, the asphyxiation in a pollution of plenty, is perhaps destined to act as a salutary brake on that rampant headlong thrust towards technological suicide now contagiously dominating the mentalities of the world's greater powers. Of all the great nations of our earth, India is the only one which might escape this vast mental and material epidemic, which has possessed men's minds, and which is spelling disaster for humanity and for all life on our planet. Perhaps India might strike a balance, which while assuring the broadening of every kind of knowledge, will steadfastly refuse and forbid its indiscriminate application, and while keeping alive and paying tribute by means of pilot plants to a technology which it finds easy to pursue, will defend the greater human needs: moral, aesthetic, cultural; it will, we hope, refuse to surrender human choice abjectly to the Gross National Product.

Moreover, by refusing to sink untold treasure into very temporary developments, such as fossil fuel, i.e. oil or atomic power, and even great dams, it will not find itself burdened with commitments and vested interests, which are an obstacle and in fact prevent the development and application of a more refined, advanced technology, which can improve the quality of human life. With her unbroken history of several thousand years, it should be easy for this great people to detect the spurious and the false, the transitory and the illusory. For India the choice must not lie between the brutal and crushing suppression of totalitarian governments, with the attendant physical and mental agony wilfully imposed by the organized state, and, on the other hand, the abuse and devaluation of liberty, become licence to manufacture, to advertise, to befoul and pollute our minds and destroy our bodies, with the attendant agonies, mental and physical, willingly and freely incurred.

India must lead us to a different path, new in terms of the dead hand of monolithic structures, bureaucratic administration, technology and commerce, in which cases reasoning is based on one overriding and usually inadequate premise; to a path which in truth is but a continuation of a long evolution which has, still today, and despite all odds, kept alive the infinitely subtle and complex wisdom which is at once synonymous with, and in harmony with life's organic processes. It cannot be for nothing that India gave the world Gandhi, who, like Jesus two thousand years ago, was killed by his own. But unlike Jesus, who was legally and officially sentenced and executed by an institution which felt itself threatened and which played upon the horrid mob, Gandhi was the victim of a fanatic—surely an anachronism in India, particularly the type which is not intolerant of violence and repression, which we all can understand, but is intolerant of non-violence, of tolerance itself. This sad type is related to the simple murderer. Only one thing I can say with certainty in this connection: artists are, generally speaking, not murderers. Gandhi spoke and lived the truth, in the Indian tradition of the living and practising saint. He was recognizably Indian, yet he held his own with the statesmen of the world. He did not address himself to one or several classes in particular, nor did he presume to lay down the law for all men for ever, but he spoke with the authority and the compassion of one who lived his faith and who knew the people he was addressing, as well as the people he was speaking about.

He had faith in the Indian villager. He knew it was the village, not the city, that was and is the backbone of India. For the living tradition is wedded to the villagers and their land, not to the new, brash and terrifying cities. His conception of the cottage industries of India will be achieved in the next round of technological application, in which the most discreet and elegant solutions will be wedded to age-old practices and forms of life, as is already happening in Switzerland, where many small villages have a compact, unirritating industry a few yards from where a farmer may be restoring his land with the precious wastes, liquid and solid, of his barnyard, as in fact in a little village my wife and I visited near Jaipur, which manufactures a finer quality paper for official requirements.

I for one will not accept as the final God-redeemer of India the noisy, smelly, uncompanionable tractor, which cannot even copulate or reproduce—no Indian temple would have been elevated to this monster. Give me Saraswati,[1] or even Hanuman,[2] any day. Theirs will still be the last word. Nor do I believe that ends justify means. Each means is an end and each end is a means. The two are inextricably wedded together.

I would rather confine discussions more modestly and realistically to pertinent purposes than to vague and misleading, even

[1] Goddess of wisdom and science.　　　　[2] A monkey-god.

dangerous, ideals or ends like peace in general, to which people pay no more than lip-service and to which they are not bound by any moral or intellectual yardstick.

We have known too many false ideals. It is not self-sacrifice which has been wanting in any age, nor has it been self-discipline. The Aztecs, the Japanese, the Christians, the Nazis even, not to speak of the Russians and the English and the Americans, including in fact our contemporary world-wide urban, rural and desert guerillas, have all drawn upon a human readiness for self-sacrifice and discipline. It is the ideals which are often suspect. Even the most altruistic sacrifice aimed at redeeming and freeing peoples around the world, though often essential, is very largely delusory. The problems are both international and local, and must be handled on both levels.

In India there is that reality which knows that so long as a man is integrated into the natural world wherein his five senses are engaged—his memory, his hands and body, his heart and mind— he will never question the reason for living, he will never doubt whether life has purpose. It may seem a paradox to many millions in the West that human life *can* have a purpose and meaning in the absence of consumer goods, and travel tours, and the obligation to pay back mortgages, but what has become a terrifying situation is this very sense of purposelessness in the face of so much temptation. Only the urge to violence survives the atrophy of other senses and instincts.

I believe that one reason for the absence of institutionalized torture and massacre in India is the blissful lack of human institutions! The recognizable living saint can only exist in a society where, like the Zadik or Holy Man in Jewish tradition, a divine order is accepted rather than a human one. It takes several hundred years for a Christian saint to be canonized, yet any Hindu or Jew can recognize a Holy Man. But he is never canonized because there is no formal institution.

Look around at all civilizations. The only great civilization without a history of organized and institutionalized torture is that of India. There is not the smallest medieval castle in Europe without its torture chamber. This people has never known that compulsion to try to alter a human being's convictions and opinions forcibly and brutally, as Catholics and Protestants, Nazis and Communists have continually done. The acceptance of a different way of life and thought is part of the Indian cosmos in which variety is sanctioned, in which sanctity is accorded to every variety. The indigenous beliefs reconcile the one with the many. Where else does this hold? Already the plague of the one way only—each group and single unit proclaiming its or his own private superiority—is reaching these shores. This low-grade madness, which is endemic to the whole world except for those who have surmounted it, and except and above all for much of India, is already gaining toeholds in this sub-continent. Its carriers are the great new urban congregations, their organized machines, political, commercial, industrial, and the machines' raw material: the unsatisfied, unfulfilled, frustrated masses. This root concept belonging to almost all civilizations and religions of owning a man, body, mind and soul, can only yield to the concept of a life belonging to and owned as it were by God, not man.

Nor should India follow in her social planning the path of the technological countries. An important section of this great nation lives on what I might call a direct economy—one almost independent of the intermediary use of money. This is the section which can cushion the poorer ranks of society and welcome the indigent with dignity.

In the other countries, the State must or should maintain everyone with money payments because lack of money, even of sufficient money, creates a total social outcast and untold misery far beyond that of the poorest Indian villager.

I have always maintained that basics, the simplest wholesome food, shelter and care should be altogether free of a price-tag.

Yet perhaps it is those very nations farthest engaged in this one-way path, as possibly the United States, which may also be the first to take the revolutionary and courageous decisions required to halt us in our present tracks and to break a new path. We are caught in the dilemma between fear on the part of the elected powers and fanaticism on the part of rebellious groups. The establishment represents the majority in the United States, and fears change and wishes to avoid sacrifice—the anarchical elements want change and are ready to sacrifice. Are we not facing the same situation within nations as we are between nations, in which the sovereign interests of one nation or of one group within a nation (even a majority) must now embrace a larger section, helping, resisting and winning over even those of whom it is afraid? It is in England where such revolutions occur most smoothly, where under the protective mantle of continuing benign traditions and institutions, privileged sections of the people can preside at the spreading of such privileges to others together with the concurrent reduction of their own. Without this characteristic, neither Britain nor the Commonwealth would have survived as the civilizing and hopeful influence they are in the world today.

Despite the travail, the tribulations, the terrifying turmoil, due in no small part to influences outside this country—I would still and always turn to India with the plea that she help us define the values we can share together, values which will rekindle trust between living beings, values worth sacrifice and struggle, and holding promise for our children's children.

We are tired of those false and narrow ideals that have proved hollow. The words sound empty and mocking. Whatever they held of brotherhood and goodness are long since perverted— the words 'democratic', 'communistic', 'socialistic', 'labour', 'capitalistic', even 'freedom' and 'liberty' have gone sour. It is because each of these wonderful conceptions was captured by a group which was determined to triumph over another 'guilty' group. Thank God, the world seems to be growing too sophisticated and cynical to swallow these any longer.

For *me* these terms *have* retained their original purity and their essential strength. I am a Communist with Jesus, a Democrat with Lincoln, a Monarchist with Asoka, a Republican with William Tell, a Theocrat with Moses, and within reason a capitalist and a socialist. I am, for instance, quite proprietary about my violins and, of course, my wife, Diana, and I hope she feels the same way about me. But I am most myself with Buddha, along with the other great B's: Bach, Beethoven, Brahms and Bartók, along with John Donne and Shakespeare, and very particularly with my wife. I believe in Liberty as practised by the disciplined and dedicated artist—a liberty which does no violence to any life. I believe in Equality as applied by an even-handed Justice and Law. I believe in Fraternity as it might perhaps exist in Heaven between the Lion and the Lamb.

A way of life which excludes the dominion of the unknown, of the mysterious, is simply untrue to life itself. The frenetic assertion of man's absolute power over nature, of his ability to direct, to dominate, the conviction that even if today he may be short of this capacity, it is surely just around the corner—this is sheer madness, it is a lie.

Deeply embedded in Indian living is a sense of universal budgeting expressed in the theory of reincarnation. Every action is reckoned, but unlike in Christian or Mohammedan doctrine, a single individual life is not considered a completed unit sufficient to earn a permanent retirement in Heaven or Hell. In the West there is the stress on individual redemption even at the expense of other lives. But in Hindu theory one lifetime is merely one instalment of the whole life, which returns for re-adjustments in further lifetimes, thus remarkably fusing heredity and merit, the two most valid criteria of natural and human selection—and certainly superior to wealth. Thus is the continuity of life-cycles from generation to generation maintained, just as the continuum between human and animal and between animal and vegetable is assured. At least this must solve the appalling problem of over-population which must by now prevail in the Christian Heaven and Hell! No wonder that under these conditions animals had to be denied souls. Yet how essential, how ennobling, how comforting can all our religions be. How wonderfully revealing of the spirit of man, of his greatest and noblest dimensions.

India must help us to define the truth which is for all, for the old and the young, for the rich and the poor, for the innocent and the guilty, the strong and the weak, for the master and the pupil, the parent and the child, for the illiterate and the literate, and for generations yet unborn.

1970

Part Four: Britain, Europe and the World

20. Cultural Influences of Empire

THERE IS without doubt grandeur about Empire, and a special nobility about the British Empire. There is a particular timeliness in investigating today the qualities and characteristics which give it contemporary meaning in its present embodiment both to itself and to the world. I know that the fashion in England is to think of 'Empire' as a fossilized relic, bereft of any current validity; and perhaps today, in the imperial capital, it is only the alien, troubadour, American violinist who can hold up a mirror reflecting not the petty, daily dissatisfactions and vicissitudes of mere existence for economic and political survival, but the great role of Britain in human terms in the perspective of world history and geography. But do not imagine that I am launching into a Kiplingesque glorification of the trappings of Empire, or of its sheer magnitude, power and glory. Of course we cannot deny that empires since ancient times deserve our respect and gratitude for offering the longest single strands of cohesion, continuity and security: periods when real values, the values of human culture, art and knowledge could be pursued. No, beauty owes much to the beast. But we tend to be mesmerized by the great and powerful, and to equate size and strength with rigid, unified structures, social, industrial, administrative, as if this size in itself were a function of the big instead of being a function of the small, in fact of the very *smallest* cell, which must remain for ever vital and healthy, the prime and indispensable source of growth, replenishment, energy and size.

There is an apposite old Chinese dictum which says something to the effect that one should never attack the already big, but rather cultivate the still small, for the big can only survive if it regenerates itself from its smallest cells. If it does not it is not only too big to attack but not even worth attacking.

It was not emperors who built the British Empire, not Caesars,

163

Kaisers or Czars. No British monarch demanded an empire, and if his ambitions happened to be too megalomaniac, he lost, as did George the Third. England's only effort to impose a permanent domination upon a neighbouring country ended rather unsuccessfully in Ireland.

No, the Empire was built by individuals (protestors, adventurers, scholars and writers, soldiers, sailors, courtiers and miscreants—rugged, romantic, practical, imaginative) and not by a despot's lackeys. It is this very loosely knit quality of the British Empire, its tremendous variety of administration within a great unity, its unwillingness to impose an iron-clad grip upon itself or its territories, which enabled this Empire to survive and to transform itself gradually into the Commonwealth, which will no doubt shortly evolve into parallel and complementary associations of nations.

Thanks to its healthy and renewed cellular growth, rather than to any rigid, rusting, crumbling structure, the Commonwealth is flexible. It can grow and bend; it does not break. It is great to the extent that it respects the diverse requirements, the indigenous social structures of its various parts. The British Empire would have been even greater had it respected and encouraged indigenous cultures even more, for it is magnanimity, compassion and wisdom that above all create the truly great associations of mankind.

This principle is extremely pertinent to our crucial instant of history; again we see the dreams of and the need for size and supra-national units, the association of human communities confused with the imposition of uniformity, sameness, rigidity of administration, conformity of laws and customs, and similarity of motives, ambitions and fantasies. This is a dangerous thought, and painful in application. Literally it implies that to achieve friendship and co-operation we must fight every inch of the way. This is, of course, something of a contradiction. It is so tiresome and discouraging to see common opinions dividing into opposing extremes or merging in a wishy-washy tepid compromise, as if the choice were for ever between those who can only see into their stomachs and maintain that eating is the only essential, and those who can only see out of their stomachs and maintain that elimination alone is essential. Or finally, the centre gets together and settles the burning issue by deciding that neither the one nor the other may be permitted!

The need for both cohesion and independence of units, for deciding the limit and responsibilities of each as well as their reciprocal activities, is greater than ever before. Instead of the harmonious function of a living community of independent people bound to a common culture, the personal concept of independence is tending to become irresponsible and self-permissive without reference to a larger context; and the common culture a mass uniformity and passivity without dignity or real conviction. The terrifying abstraction of sheer numbers, the multiplication games of industry and commerce, the impersonal and anonymous quality of modern science on the one hand, and on the other the starvation and repression of the individual human being's needs and instincts for guidance and support, strength and well-being, fulfilment and discrimination, faith and conviction, and their cynical betrayal by cheap, debased, mass-produced substitutes, leave the community group sadly abandoned by both the mass and the individual, by both the abstract and the personal, by both knowledge and art. In fact, art and knowledge are no longer the expressions of a community culture; they represent a civilization, not a *community*.

My argument is that a culture, including art and wisdom for the community group to share, cannot exist without a real communal responsibility, together with almost infinite variety. It cannot exist without the increased autonomy of the smallest groups, communities, right down to the individual. In other words, art and wisdom, I am convinced, can have value and meaning for a person or persons only to the extent that the human mind concerned retains its individual independence, autonomy and responsibility. It is difficult to imagine a domesticated pet having independent volition or opinion: it licks th hand that feeds it and, if well-trained, will bite the stranger.

Today, because of the weakening of the will of the smaller units, the family, the village, the city-state, the biggest units are less able to insure or protect the survival of man than ever before. I see no real contradiction between regional movements for greater autonomy—as for instance the Welsh and the Scottish 'National' movements—and the simultaneous widening of world unity and cohesion. In fact, one cannot proceed without the other, any more than a balanced society can exist without a sense of the freedom and independence of the individual belonging to that society.

I often wonder how many of us today would have the will, the imagination, and the conviction to re-establish democracy were it destroyed, by fighting for it, inch by inch, as our fore-fathers did. For it can be best defended in small, independent communities, tailored to man-size: communities in which the voice of single men and women can be heard. It is largely because empires of the past could not possibly control the thought or satisfy all the needs of their populations from a central authority (and not through lack of trying), that pockets of self-government, islanders, mountaineers, monasteries and city-states were left to establish democracy. The British Empire was great because no British government could ever dominate its own home country!

Let us remember this lesson today as we are engaged in forming new and yet closer associations of nations. The common culture of the European nations arises from the fact that, facing out to sea on three sides from their peninsula, with Britain surrounded by sea, they have never long accepted a hegemony of any one nation from within their ranks, and never from without—hence France's great effort to resist the cultural impact (the con-temporary form of colonization) of the USA. To remain true to the essence of European culture and tradition, to fulfil its great destiny to the utmost, we must respect the inherent independence and diversity of the smallest region, while at the same time defining those areas of common interest and united achievement that belong to the superstate of Europe. But ours and theirs is a two-pronged effort, for unless the national governments can divest themselves of responsibilities, and shed every superfluous admini-strative function that can be performed better at regional and community levels, these national governments, by the same token, will never be able to achieve the whole-hearted co-operation of their peoples required to create the greater units—we hope ultimately, the greatest unit—of world association.

Only if we can make progress along the broad human front by means of a two-pronged drive, returning to the individual and the smallest community a measure of the autonomy, dignity and independence that form a counterpart to the integration achieved for the largest and eventually the very largest unit, can we in this privileged part of the world fulfil the role and the destiny expected of us by the billions of our suffering and hopeful fellow-men. Throughout the world humanity is waiting for a lead, for an example of nations being able to get together—independent nations who have never bowed their heads and those who have always had pride in their own background and their own culture. If these nations could get together on the basis of their own character and their own history, and make a working association, it would provide the world with the greatest inspiration, and I am sure would lead the way, eventually, to a truly civilized world.

This is the cultural influence, this is the heritage of Empire that we must cherish and ever renew. The fact that the British could administer India with a handful of people has always struck me as an extraordinary phenomenon. And it was only because they had respect for the living organism. Just as every Englishman respects plants, trees, flowers and animals and his fellow-men, so too, when he came to a very strange country, he left as much of it alone as he possibly could and saw to it that it somehow worked together. It is this administrative example, the parliamentary example, the example of things working together towards a common harmony, that has enabled India to survive until now; and let us hope that as an independent nation she will continue to build on this very precious example of co-operation. Other nations and other peoples with a different background go in with a bulldozer and enormous power, and feel they must remake everything in their own image. I think that is wrong. And that is all the more reason why I feel that the example of the British Commonwealth can still serve a useful purpose today as it changes and evolves. I hate to see (and I can say so as a foreigner) the throwing away of heritages merely because the new is the fashion or the new is important. The new *is* important, but the new can only fulfil itself in the bodies that we were born with. We cannot throw away our body and decide to be a new person. If we want to be something new we have to look after the old that we have inherited.

LONDON, 1967

21. A Vision of Europe

IN VIEW OF the tremendous importance of the 'vision of Europe', entertained by so many through several thousand years—emperors, tyrants, popes and idealists—and recalling the disappointment of the great violinist Bronislav Hubermann, who between the two world wars was one of 'Europe's' most dedicated advocates, I believe it is as important to list the pitfalls of union as it is to stress the advantages to be gained.

NEGATIVE FACTORS

Union implies a dynamic equilibrium attained and maintained between what is held in common on the one hand and what is held in exclusivity on the other. Where this delicate and dynamic balance is absent, i.e. where the elements of dependence and independence are not in equilibrium, common dreams, hopes, needs, fears, and suffering hardly engender a community of interests unless agreement is reached on some identifiable villain, some scapegoat, or some well-defined common objective. This objective in turn finds its expression in a leader, who must inevitably be to some extent a withholder, for in return for promises of future salvation he must withhold present satisfactions; he only wields power before and during crises, before and during war, and is discarded or eliminated as soon as possible thereafter.

Prosperity among technologically advanced societies seemed just such a likely and tempting objective, especially so long as Western Europe, as one entity, sick and afraid of new destruction, was bent on reconstruction, for which she needed peace, and was galvanized between the polarity of American support and Russian ruthlessness.

However, for the common man national prosperity is no longer an issue so long as his individual security, freedom, and money for daily needs and wants are guaranteed. 'Prosperity' *per se* is gaining a certain taint in that it now stands for more pollution, more ugliness, more weapons, more callousness, more individual debtors mortgaging their uncertain future. Then 'Whose prosperity?' it is asked in England: 'The prosperity of the French farmer at my expense?' The lure of prosperity alone, the promise of a higher rate of annual growth, are poor bets. Higher ideals, nobler common purposes, even greater fears are required.

Among those who would advocate union there remain a number to whom this signifies merely a forceful imposition of the stronger upon the weaker, a form of rape that has happened endlessly and is frequently happening still in the lands of Europe.

Great Britain has blissfully escaped this brutality for one thousand years. The European nations have so often fallen prey to dictatorships, and it is understandable that, having pursued her own path so well and consistently these many centuries, Great Britain hesitates to ally herself formally to the uneasy republics and tyrannies of Europe. A union along the mature lines of the three Scandinavian countries, wherein each retains its independence, its King, its economy, is the kind of union to which Britain might conceivably adhere.

We speak of a common Judeo-Christian spirituality. If this historical, biblical seed had borne any fruit in terms of brotherliness and support, it should have been impossible for Hitler to have arisen, nor would the persecution of Jews have found such ripe and ready ground from Russia and Poland through Germany, France and Spain. And again, had such great religions as the Mohammedan and the Judaic, also sprung from a common source, had power over men's hearts and minds, would we be witnessing the present tragedy in the Middle East? After all, it was under Mohammedan rule that Spain achieved her highest level of tolerance and elegance and the Jews there their greatest intellectual flowering. Today we see Catholics and Protestants fighting again as of old. Cain and Abel were brothers. . . .Then again, does Europe, with its many regions and races, its myriad languages and dialects in their fantastic variety, and the Europeans with their ingrained habits and reflexes of fear, suspicion and violence, really share anything more than this fear that actually divides them? Europe is after all a peninsula, a great confluence of the Western drift of Eurasia. Going for ever westwards, the various tribes tumbled over each other, carving little toeholds before succumbing in turn to the next wave. It took many hundreds of years before accumulated waves could bridge the Atlantics.

If we all fear a common enemy, or suspect a common evil, we share something, however negative. But if we fear and suspect each other, what hope is there then? Perhaps the spirit of a united whole is strongest in the enslaved countries behind the Iron Curtain, to the extent that those sad peoples can focus on an outside enemy. But part of Russia is to all intents and purposes still European, and Europe has generally been beaten and defaced by other Europeans. We speak of high-minded purpose and a European conception of the dignity of man, yet Europe hardly lifted a finger as an entity to defend these rights. I cannot believe that more prosperity on the one hand and high-sounding words on the other can be a substitute for the real unity of conviction that finds its expression in some kind of action.

For those who have left Europe far behind—North and South Americans, South Africans—it does represent an entity. But not to a European. Even the British speak somewhat disparagingly of their own Commonwealth: this I find extremely depressing. The Commonwealth is the only international association of nations sharing a common attitude to the dignity of man, a common language and common ancestry. I feel it is tragic that the motherland should view it with less respect, with a shrunken appraisal of the great example it is and of its unique function, than the millions of Commonwealth subjects all over the world, many of whom consider it the most precious association they have. Ours is a sad age, which does not exclude the possibility of its being a hopeful one: an age when people search for the essence of life, its ecstasies, beatitude and peace, and when they find only the violation of life, violence and war. When I view the future pessimistically, I can only see pestilence and famine and the apocalypse. The actual future may go one way or the other, or it may be a combination of or a combat between both.

That other great supra-national association, the Church of Rome, is not likely to be the fountain-head of national or political unions again.

POSITIVE FACTORS

I regret being so negative in my appraisal of the vision of a united Europe; however, I do perceive some positive elements in the picture. The international brotherhood of young people is for the first time a force in history. A new universal philosophy is being hammered out in the face of the inescapable facts, the inexorable fate awaiting them today. For the most part the young people realize the complex interdependence of all acts, the infinite repercussions of thoughts and behaviour. A new morality, a new philosophy are implicit in the recognition of unity; an impatience with the hypocrisy that disassociates and isolates one act from another; a concern with total ecology, including man; a perspective on the relationship of past and future: these are aspects of their evolving thought-forms. Young people are also aware of the infinite diversity of cultures. Fashions in music, dance, painting and the stage are now continually drawing upon exotic inspiration. Politically, they are ready to implement these convictions, even at the cost of changing those systems that seem to be unable to take the drastic measures needed, or honestly to discuss the *real* problems of our era.

I could say much more of the imagination and the integrity of our younger generations. Obviously many fall by the wayside through drugs, others are impelled to indiscriminate violence, still others are stupid or narrow-minded, and reject every restraint while seizing every opportunity of behaving irresponsibly; but by and large there is real value and real hope in a large proportion of our young.

Optimistically, I see us upon the threshold not of a more prosperous and luxurious society, but rather on the threshold of greater physical controls and greater spiritual and artistic freedom; of a science geared more to knowledge than to commerce; of a commerce which, although committed to the freedom of supply and demand and exchange, is severely circumscribed as to its wastages and its influences. Perhaps life itself may yet gain a value approximating that of money and power.

I see a need for symbols of human achievement and dignity, human symbols expressed by the various arts, a greater compassion and a larger tolerance.

Who will be the new Charlemagne?

For our high convictions to be protected, they require some embodiment. As Lord Coleraine has written: progress is the result of the 'gradual dissemination of exceptional excellence' in every field, and not of the arbitrary levelling of all differences. Europe has had and still has a tremendous reserve, a vast accumulation of 'exceptional excellence'. This is its priceless heritage. Above all, Europe has a depth of human experience upon which it should draw in maturity and a spirit of true philosophy. It is still too close to its own painful recent experiences to reason in any other terms than those of retaliation against all who caused the endless tragedy and suffering. The European may still be too primitive: the German, the French villager, the English provincial, for instance, is often too prejudiced and narrow-minded to put his experience to constructive use. This evolution of excellence can only come from the young, and the exceptional.

An international political party addressing itself primarily to the young, but unlike the Nazi youth, only along the principles I mentioned, could do a great deal to bring about that harmony in diversity, that union with variety, that is our common aim. It is perhaps above all important to keep alive every form of co-operation between the peoples. The great minds in all countries must be free to meet, to discuss and to exchange their ideas and convictions. We must press for this with the peoples in dominated countries as well, using every device of encouragement, temptation and threat. There should be meetings to discuss international inspection, international law and justice. All countries should strive to develop common objectives such as the preservation of the countryside, a United Europe, and World Government compatible with a *variety* of governments.

Of course, the Common Market is already in being: it need not be created; the club exists and it is only a matter of joining. Already in such joint projects as the Concorde and no doubt many other adventures the path is being prepared. Great Britain, as the most politically stable member, the most mature, powerful, and with the most international links, would naturally have the most to contribute and the greatest responsibility. Without Great Britain the Common Market will only be a trading association and will never achieve the status of an organic and integrated super-power; the 'vision of Europe' will remain a pipe-dream.

HOPES

Federation or Union *should* represent the gradual dissolution of national units, those antediluvian concepts that force a multitude of different elements, each with a different area of association, into one mould—the national one (the very symbol of coercion and suppression). This dissolution would, in truth, release the variety of regional expressions—linguistic, stylistic, cultural, agricultural, artistic—hitherto held imprisoned in the one national mould. In a Federation the old lines of demarcation would be irrelevant; but protection would be afforded by a larger body.

We are mistaken in thinking that future Federation will inevitably be in terms of nation-states. This is a fallacy: only in the case of Great Britain and New Zealand, Australia, Iceland, etc., does this hold good, in which instances a natural ocean-boundary, not a man-made one, is drawn. Common interests normally overlap national boundaries; climate, topography, soil, altitude, vegetation, disease, language, even the stamping grounds of wild life, the needs of gipsies, migrant or primitive peoples, and so on, each correspond to a different territorial pattern.

Who can pretend that fixed national frontiers do not continually crack, and that the new African States have not been formed within arbitrary lines drawn at various periods by European cartographers who probably had no conception of the character of the regions they were carving out, and in any case were not in a position to exercise independent judgement? They covered Africa in many parts with a right-angle grid running N–S and E–W, in the same way as the unimaginative, blocked minds in Washington D.C. laid out a grid for states, counties and cities and all property in the United States of America. So the towns have become open-ended caverns, down which either the north wind or the east wind blows. Sometimes the winds meet to create a whirlwind. The result, quite rightly, is that now in Freudian terms they speak of man's need for the womb. If we wish to avoid continuous wars, we must dissolve rigid, fixed frontiers and substitute new 'district' frontiers, overlapping and fluid.

The largest unit, the administration encompassing, say, the whole peninsula of Europe, would protect all of its different member units (a) from each other, and (b) from outsiders. Europe offers good material to achieve this solution. Until quite recently it has known independent city-states, independent small kingdoms, as in Italy and in Germany. It could recreate these entities without too much trouble. A proper equilibrium can only be created by opposing the single to the numerous. Can this happen voluntarily? Can we move step by step towards a definite goal? Switzerland has in fact achieved this very triumph. Or can it only happen after the breakdown of the present national European states?

The great vision is that of the progress of a nucleus of whole-some cells, exhibiting the right degrees and proportions of firm-ness and flexibility, creating by example, influence and interest an ever-larger association of congenial bodies.

The Commonwealth provides a good beginning. Scandinavian association is certainly another possibility. An English-speaking and Atlantic Union, the Common Market, and European Union are others. How far is humanity now from that heaven of World Government, of harmony between peoples! How sad it is to think of a great civilization like China's as an enemy! One wonders when, and if in our own or our children's lifetime a mutual trust and respect will somehow come into being.

Yet I believe that we are now evolving a body of common doctrine with regard to values, to the cycle and re-cycle of existence, to the economy of cycles, to the respect for all life, to the requirements of a healthy environment, to the relative functions of an education, in fact of the many educations required (not by any means only that of literacy); and a body of the common knowledge essential to all people.

These evolving attitudes, these new insights, these truths are creating the equivalent of a new religion, which will one day sweep the world. This 'religion' will fulfil what past religions have simply pointed to—man as a responsible element in the total presence of *all* life, of the whole universe and of an infinite span of time. Without this accompanying belief and faith, common markets and alliances of every kind will only have a limited value. These deep-held convictions, held already by many and notably many young people, must not only be shared, but practised. Just as in economics a home market is essential to build a great industry, so the cadres, the disciplines, the experience and practices required to administer the new structures vital for humanity's survival will have to be applied, developed and perfected on home ground.

Again I turn to the affiliation of Britain, Holland and the Scandinavian lands as offering the best beginnings for those extra-Commonwealth associations between different nations and races that may become the foundation of a World Society.

1970

22. *West Berlin*

FIRST OF ALL, a few questions. When we speak of the German people, what do we have in mind? Are we to imagine everyone who uses the German language—that is, the inhabitants of Austria, Czechoslovakia, Alsace and German Switzerland—or are we to conceive of the German people as a collection of culturally independent and heterogeneous principalities, as they were until 1870? Or are they indeed the united and indivisible people who submitted more or less willingly to Prussian militarism and to a mystique of national destiny and superiority?

Can we as human beings of Slavic, Jewish, Gipsy and German background trust our fate to a completely self-determined nation too easily led astray by its obsession for an abstract and often biased mental and physical tidiness?

Other than aggressive ones, what *national* achievements and *national* memories does 'Germany' have in the worlds of music, literature, and science, which she would not have had in any case in a non-national context?

No 'national' problem, Jewish, Korean, Algerian, Congolese, West Berliner or any other, can any longer be solved with the outdated, primitive and one-dimensional concept of national boundaries or national self-determination. National boundaries are only one—and that one the crudest—criterion of area and population units.

I believe it would be a mistake to bend every effort towards the useless, psychologically and emotionally dangerous object of so-called national self-determination, at the expense of first trying to improve the human being in himself and in all his existing and various associations and ideals, as well as improving the fundamental structure of the United Nations and other such human associations. In that way all free and natural associations of no matter what size and shape—be they of geography, culture, taste, or whatever—can all flourish equally and simultaneously.

I have the greatest admiration and sympathy for the people of West Berlin, who have endured a great deal and who have shown steadfastness and perhaps the greatest political awareness in our day of any population. On the other hand, are the people of West Berlin more deserving of self-determination than the people of East Berlin, or of East Germany, or Poland, or Hungary, or Peru? Or more deserving than those Germans who were designated as Jews by a previous régime, and were certainly not accorded any self-determination?

Of course I would like to see every individual and every group free to express itself, with its own way of life, but my main point is that unless we start first by defending other people's self-determination, whatever self-determination we may achieve for ourselves is of a very ephemeral and insecure nature, likely to be destroyed at the first wave of chance.

In my opinion there is only one constructive solution to the Berlin problem. The West Berliners should, I think, say something like this:

'It is for us, the West Berliners, to take the initiative to determine our fate within the context of what is possible and what is morally right.

'Let us face the fact that Berlin is dead and discredited as a national capital. In the past as a capital city it was the seat of Prussian and later of Nazi arrogance, and it is now the administrative centre of an amputated vassal state. As for us, and as for West Berlin, we have simply become a bone of contention between great powers—a pawn likely to be sacrificed—a source of dangerous friction, an irritation in the fabric of mankind.

'In the past, capitals of vanquished states were razed to the ground, as Carthage was. Today, mankind has advanced somewhat—they are razed *before* defeat. But we still retain the privilege of making our contribution to world peace. We can still lift a hand to help our neighbours.

'We therefore forfeit and relinquish our political union with Bonn, which is technically difficult to reconcile with the four- or three-power status of this city, and difficult to implement in view of the geographical situation.

'We wish to identify ourselves with our fellow-citizens of East

Berlin, who have suffered in recent years more than we have, and to declare our intention of becoming together with them the first truly free city, West and East Berlin united—a city unattached to any single state, depending for its security on the co-operation of powers, not on their stubbornness. As we are anyway at the mercy of the great powers, we would rather rely on their joint sense of historical and human responsibility than on their competing rivalries.

'We wish to break down barriers, not to build them, and this we know cannot be achieved on unilateral terms. We wish to bring Americans, Russians, British and French together again, and make them shoulder their collective responsibilities as human beings.

'We have as yet insufficient faith that the United Nations alone can defend us, so that until that day comes we would wish a parallel joint assurance of the great powers, together with a token *integrated* police force comprising all four. Our condition is that the city be reunited, all sectors together, and free.

'Only in this way would we be fulfilling our historical debts and duties. Only in this way would we be making an important and real contribution to the security and peace of the world. Thus only might Berlin become the healthy core around which might grow an ever larger association of free peoples and true world citizens.'

1962

23. India and the Way to Peace

AT BEST, violence can never serve as a positive example. It leaves the victim bent on the destructive passions of revenge and hate; and it too often leaves the perpetrator with a sense of unrestricted power, unaccountable to any higher power of reason, uncontrolled by self-restraint, a cancerous element in the social body.

In contrast, by turning the other cheek, as in Mahatma Gandhi's non-violent or passive resistance campaign, we achieve more positive and lasting results. Firstly, the violence of the attack is absorbed instead of being returned, as the impact of a stone would be absorbed when thrown into a pool; secondly, we deny the aggressor the satisfaction of superiority; thirdly, we provide a good example for emulation; fourthly, we have maintained a sense of proportion. The most important achievement is that we have interrupted what is called a vicious circle.

DIFFERENT ATTITUDES

I believe both aggressive and passive attitudes have their proper place and time. The eye-for-an-eye and tooth-for-a-tooth approach is useful as an emergency device (for instance when attacked by a wild animal), but can have no lasting effect.

Actually, we all partake concurrently of both attitudes in certain degrees. From the point of view of survival, both are equally valid—the one in the immediate and finite, the other in continuity and in the practical application to our existence of the eternal and infinite; the one where life is divided against itself and where a single, unique, and finite reward must be won, and where for right or wrong reasons antagonism has ruled out the sense of fraternity or the possibility of conciliation; the other wherever a harmonious society is being produced and maintained, as for many thousands of years in India, and as must sooner or later happen on a scale to include all humanity, all nations, races and creeds.

It is customary to call the 'eye-for-an-eye' and 'tooth-for-a-tooth' approach realistic; the other, which involves turning the other cheek, idealistic, visionary, and impractical.

Poverty, chastity and obedience are not for nothing universally recognized (in both East and West) as the hallmarks of godliness, but even these citadels of virtue have been stormed by vanity, pride, prejudice and arrogance, when the purity of the objective was not commensurate with the stringent means to reach it. When these unnatural rigours are submitted to and practised only to gain personal ascendancy (which is the unforgivable sin of spiritual pride) or when they are so exaggerated as to suppress powerful urges without sublimating or otherwise releasing them, these measures defeat their own purpose. (In India, these self-denials are not expected of a man until quite late in life, for, according to the natural and sensitive Buddhist traditions, there is a time and place for everything.)

THE HIGHEST ENDS

Nowhere is the pursuit of holiness more a living and a crucial matter than it is in India. It seems to correspond to the American individual's inalienable right to the pursuit of happiness, which has become, I am afraid, in a large measure but the pursuit of pleasure.

In India, too, any individual, of whatever stratum, unsponsored by any organized body, religious, civil or commercial, may start on his lonely path to holiness; nor need he await canonization to receive the homage of his followers.

All that this solitary human being is assured of in India, is, on the one hand, the respect and sympathy, the understanding and charity of his fellow-men, and on the other, for himself, an unimpeded path to increasing purity and the succeeding stages of union with God. He may beg but once a day, at the first house he meets in the village, and must then deposit half his food at the temple outside the village for others poorer than he before he may serve himself. The holy man of India is, therefore, not the common beggar of urban life; he is traditionally a selfless and dedicated person, severely restricted by his self-discipline, not allowed to demand or receive from society more than the pittance required for survival, as would a tree or a flower from air and water. He is looked up to as an example of human virtue and of the renunciation of material for spiritual values. He is a constant reminder to the people of the highest ends and the highest motives in life.

The Indians are a people naturally philosophical rather than dynamic. They do not confine themselves to crystallization and finality in art or science, and prefer a regulated fluidity to some unique triumphal achievement. In music, too, they prefer the improvised to the crystallized; they are for ever cultivating the proper mood, the appropriate state of mind and body in which to create, to receive inspiration, and thus they achieve such inner stillness as to be moved by the slightest stir of the divine presence.

ART AND SCIENCE

Indian art is traditional and timeless; though supremely rhythmical it is sophisticated, embellished and ornate. No fixed time limit dominates its flow, and it has no finality. It is elusive and subjective, summoned out of the void, uniting in characteristic fashion both the erotic and the spiritual.

The Indians are not particularly attracted to aggressive competitive sports, though indeed they do excel at cricket and polo; nor have they devised such machines as the steam engine or the jet aeroplane. But, paradoxically enough, in atomic science and nuclear physics they are most distinguished, as these sciences share their basic principles with the ancient tenets of the unity of all matter and its interchangeability. Nuclear science has brought us back to those ancient revelations of the microscopic homogeneity within the unity of all matter, restoring the grand conception overriding the compartmentalization of time and space, and in doctrine that are so characteristic of our Western Christian thought.

THE INDIAN VILLAGE

In contemplating the microcosm of the Indian village—its aesthetic, aristocratic and moral qualities—we discover the effects and see the results of millenia of an almost unbroken continuity of civilization based on an inspired and pre-Christian moral and ethical conception. One is inclined to regard these people as innocent, as being still partly illuminated by the last rays of the Garden of Eden, still clothed in the very first and simplest garb. For these reasons the Indian village is to me something infinitely touching and moving.

The Indian village seems singularly free from divisions, innocent of unbridgeable chasms, for over the ages time and fate and the will of the Lord have directed all the essential functions of man in an unchanging society—functions which otherwise, in our modern world, are the products of direct and arbitrary intervention.

The reconciliation of modern arbitrary behaviour with the reality of natural growth is, of course, one of the lessons that mankind still has to learn.

1959

24. The World Citizen

LET US LOOK into the future first, and see what the world citizen of the year 5000 may be. And then we shall see in what ways we can begin to take the various stages that lead to that ultimate.

For one thing I think he will be much too wise to allow himself to be labelled. He may agree to a great many different definitions, but he will never agree to *one*. He will not be a Mohammedan who is out to enslave the world to the will of Allah. And he won't be a Christian who is out to put the world in the shadow of the cross. And he won't be a capitalist who is somewhat too proud of the flood of good things he has released and distributed. And he won't be a Communist—too dogmatic with his fanatical catechism, and in his readiness to ally with the devil for the sake of the millenium. And to allay your fears I should say that this time he will not even be a Jew. He might conceivably be a violinist, if such still exist.

He will not be a one-dimensional being. After all, in the past every animal had to fend for itself and there was no one else to fight for it. Every group of animals in every species, and among humans in more recent times groups such as the coal-miners, had to fend for themselves because no one else bothered about them. The Mohammedans had to and the Christians had to. And because man takes upon himself a universal soul, he has always clothed this instinct for self-preservation in very high-sounding names, in words that would imply that he was defending mankind itself. In truth he was just having to defend himself or his group. But as soon as he becomes a four-dimensional being, so to speak, in terms of our modern world, in terms of the electronic computers that can think of a thousand different factors at one time, then he is no more just the coal-miner, the Christian, the Jew, the Communist, the capitalist—or whatever he may be called. He is not labelled exclusively any more. As soon as he acquires these other dimensions he is beginning to be a world citizen. He is able to take upon himself responsibilities beyond himself, and that, I think, is one of the chief criteria of a world citizen.

Let me define the four dimensions I have in mind. I am not speaking merely of the spatial dimensions of science. In terms of man himself I would take as my first dimension time in all its degrees. In other words, historically man must be responsible and conscious. He must view himself as a link in a long chain, responsible for the links of the past as well as for those of the future, not free to destroy either the past or the future, or to look upon anything as subject-matter for his whim and his fancy. He must, therefore, be conscious of the dimension of time, not only in its extremities of great antiquity and very far-distant future, but in all its degrees as it affects his movements and thoughts from moment to moment.

Secondly, man has to be aware of space. In other words, he lives within geographical space. But not in terms of frozen frontiers, which again offer only one criterion—one label, one nationhood, one statehood—which is already something entirely *passé*, primitive, and no longer applicable to the modern world. He must be aware of space in all its various degrees. That is, beginning with the space of his room, of his home, of his city, of the times he has with those who speak the same language, of those who share the same culture, of those who share the same weather, of those who share the same tastes—all of which may be different one from another in terms of geographical divisions. It would be absurd to assume that all of these different relationships are necessarily comprehended within one arbitrary national boundary.

Thirdly, man must be aware of all creation, of all the manifestations of life. He is responsible for them. In other words, the idea that everything is created subject to man and that man alone has a soul is no longer sufficient. No, if man is stronger and wiser and more educated than other beings he may become custodian, but not tyrant over everything else. In other words, he becomes custodian of those who are less well educated, less well favoured, and of all manifestations of life—of the tree in the forest, of the fish in the sea, and of the insects, on all of whom our life depends.

We cannot go on using them—abusing them, exploiting them—as we have until now. We shall not continue to do that with impunity. We must become aware of all living things—aware of creation.

And the fourth dimension is humanity itself. That is, the integrity with which we conduct our own lives; the persistence with which we try to purify our own thoughts, our own bodies, our own immediate environment; the desire we have to express ourselves, to perfect ourselves, to bring out the best that is within us; the respect that we must have for ourselves, of which matter we are also only custodians.

I would therefore say that he must be a four-dimensional man, this world citizen. And he will have to take his place among all these things and not allow any of them to dominate any other. He will be in harmony, in rhythm with all things, even though there will be at least four rhythms. I say four, but there will be four hundred, because any one of the rhythms can be subdivided within itself. Yet he will be able to balance all of these things together and take his example from the truth that is now being discovered by science, as well as from the truth that has always been known by the very great men of the past—such as Lâo-Tsze, Buddha, Jesus, and so many others.

I am against our accepting one label. We reduce wild life in Africa to terms of hunted meat or skins. That is hardly right. The Germans thought of a great portion of their nation as Jews, and defined them in much the same way. In other words, we cannot think of human beings simply as whatever may be edible, saleable, usable, reducible, exploitable or redeemable, about them. There is no single, simple description of anything. We cannot glibly use words such as Imperialist, or Communist.

How then can this world citizen evolve, in a world that is apparently so hostile to these various thoughts I am describing? Consider the United Nations, which has admittedly taken a great step forward in world history, and is an essential meeting-place of every label we have come to know. The boundaries that define its constituent nations are for the most part only one criterion of identity, in terms of the many manifold qualities of human beings. What is the Congo? What is Algeria? What for that matter is Israel, or Poland, or West Berlin? Is it reasonable to assume that the boundaries of these areas are perfect, God-willed, and that they are going to last for ever? We have lived long enough to learn that, even in our own short life, history has marched a thousand times more quickly than it has ever marched before, and we have seen that these boundaries were the results of arbitrary mistakes, pride, fear; of a great many bad things and a very few good ones. We cannot speak of a world citizen in one breath, and defend such boundaries in another. They are not sufficiently valid bases on which to build a human administration, or a Parliament. The Parliament of the world, or any Parliament for that matter, must be a body—an institution—that is ready to accept and to guide change. It must be ready to follow and understand pressures and to accept them. It cannot be bound by the frozen icebergs that these boundary concepts represent.

I speak of icebergs, because they melt. And when they melt and break, they break up into a great many small icebergs, and then we have splintered icebergs, and then what happens to the Prime Minister of Floe no 3? And what happens to his penguins and his fish, poor man? So you see that an institution that is to represent the world must be ready to represent it in all its aspects and must therefore be multi-dimensional. Until the Parliament of Man at any level includes the custodians of all man's dependants, and everything that is at his mercy, until it includes representatives of rivers and oceans and the air, and the wild life, and representatives of all his activities—art, science, medicine, philosophy, morality, commerce too, and all the other aspects of civilized life —it would be altogether premature to speak of a world citizen or even of an adult, civilized world. To sum up, I should like to suggest that we need to accept a four-dimensional basis to our morality, our ideology, our life, and our responsibility. And to the extent that any one person applies even a small part of this attitude to life in his dealings with his friends, his relations, his neighbours, or anyone with whom he associates, he will be preparing himself and the world for the day of the world citizen. He will have no need for labels, for labels mean wars—especially holy ones.

Now let us lower our sights, and see whether in the immediate future any application of these ideas may be at all practical and possible.

Some of these icebergs may melt, and others may join up. Until now every nation has dreamt its own dreams, each one thought that it alone, above all others, would be the dominator of the world, would unify it in its own image. The Romans thought that they would unify the world. The Germans thought *they* would. Other nations have thought so too. It has all been mistaken idealism—or perhaps greed. The Communists imagined that they would unify the world under one label. But few rational people believe that such a thing is possible today. We know already that no one nation will achieve this task. I think that this is going to be the important thought in the world. Every great nation, even the greatest iceberg in the world, realizes that it cannot dominate the scene. And therefore it will help them to join up with other icebergs, and certainly there is a great deal to be said for this. These icebergs have quite a lot in common. We must not make the mistake of thinking that Soviet Russia's Communism is something utterly alien to us. If we look back we will realize that it is simply another branch of the Christian tree—a branch of the old Judeo-Christian faith. One important concept of this tradition is that God made man to dominate the universe: he was the only one who had a soul. Well, this mistaken, one-dimensional, primitive, flat-earth concept is still characteristic of this latest branch of the Christian tree.

This tree began several thousand years ago with the Jewish universality of vision. Then, the Christian Church branched into the Church of Rome, Eastern and Western; then came another branch, the Protestant; and then a new concept—curiously enough expounded by Jews as well (Karl Marx and Trotsky)—broke away to form another branch of Judeo-Christian ideology.

So both civilizations have a great deal in common ideologically, but in addition they share the Western European culture, with a love of music and of literature. They also have in common the fact that their populations are now being educated to the new world, to the modern world, more quickly than any others in this scientific age. And this is going to be the real test of our world: that is, to what extent every one of us is going to be representative of the knowledge, the truth, the new dimensions, the new horizon, which man is now exploring.

So there is a lot to be said for the fusion of icebergs. I don't even call it co-existence—I'd go beyond that. I feel that only by recognizing every aspect of humanity can man be free to develop each single aspect within its own boundary; in other words, only those who seek and love their own culture can unite within that culture. But on each level we have a different unit, a different region of which to conceive.

If man will not emerge into this new stage of evolution that is awaiting him, he will simply fall back into barbarism for ever.

1962

Index

acoustics, 148
Africa (and Africans), 10, 13, 18, 35, 39, 45, 69, 70, 72, 86, 106, 107, 173, 185; *see also* Negroes
Algeria, 176, 185
Alsace, 176
amateur, the, 18–19
America (and Americans), *see* South America, U.S.A.
Arabs, 153
Archimedes, 114
architecture and town planning, 86, 115, 118–20, 139, 146, 147–50, 151
art, 110–32, 139, 148, 151, 181, 186
Asian Music Circle, 72
Asoka, 159
audience, the, 19, 20–22, 23, 26, 49
Australia, 173
Austria, 18, 176
Aztecs, 157

Bach, Johann Sebastian, 37, 51, 53–5, 60, 61, 65, 71, 73, 75, 101, 104, 126, 159
Bali, 12, 69
Bartók, Bela, 12, 20, 21, 22, 27, 37, 51, 56–9, 60, 64, 70, 74, 104, 124, 126, 159
Beethoven, Ludwig van, 2, 26, 27, 37, 40–44, 55–6, 75, 96, 103, 124, 159
Belgium, 169
de Bériot, Charles, 2
Bhabha, Homi, 151
Bloch, Ernest, 21, 27
Botticelli, Sandro, 124

Brahms, Johannes, 27, 75, 159
Brazil, 22
Britain (and the British), 94, 97, 120, 142, 163, 169, 172, 173, 175, 178
British Broadcasting Corporation, 47–9
British Commonwealth, 163–7, 170, 174
Britten, Benjamin, 22, 70
Brunner, Emil, 114
Buddha (and Buddhism), 114, 129, 159, 180, 185

cadenza, the, 26–7
Canada, 12
'canned' music, 14, 148
Capitalism (and capitalists), 39, 83, 138, 159, 183
Casals, Pablo, 49, 63–6
'cello, the, 64–5
Charlemagne, 172
China, 21, 71, 122, 129, 138, 152, 153, 163, 174
Chopin, Fryderyk, 51
Christianity (and Christians), 81, 83, 138, 157, 160, 169, 170, 181, 183, 187; *see also* Jesus Christ
cinema, 21, 75
Coleraine, Lord, 172
Collins, Canon John, 1
Common Market, 168–75
Commonwealth, *see* British Commonwealth
Communism (and Communists), 39, 83, 138, 145, 157, 159, 183, 184, 187

189